The Ottoman Army
1683-1732

BY
LUIGI MARSIGLI

TRANSLATED BY
G.F. NAFZIGER

The Ottoman Army
1683-1732

BY
LUIGI MARSIGLI

TRANSLATED BY
G.F. NAFZIGER

Original Edition:
THE HAGUE
Pierre Gosse & Jean Neaulme
1732

This edition:

The Ottoman Army 1683 - 1732 by Luigi Marsigli
Translated by G. F. Nafziger
Cover image by Angel Pinto
This edition published in 2025

The Nafziger Collection is an imprint of

Winged Hussar Publishing, LLC
1525 Hulse Rd, Unit 1
Point Pleasant, NJ 08742

Copyright © Winged Hussar Publishing
ISBN PB 978-1-958872-78-9
ISBN EB 978-1-958872-79-6

Index created via [Created with **TExtract** / www.TExtract.com]

Bibliographical References and Index
1. History. 2. Ottoman Empire. 3. Renaissance

Winged Hussar Publishing, LLC All rights reserved
For more information
Visit us at www.whpsupplyroom.com

Twitter: WingHusPubLLC
Facebook: Winged Hussar Publishing LLC

This book is sold subject to the condition that it shall not, by way of trade or otherwise, be lent, resold, hired out, or otherwise circulated without the publisher's prior consent in any form of binding or cover other than that in which it is published and without a similar condition, including this condition, being imposed on the subsequent purchaser.

The scanning, uploading, and distribution of this book via the Internet or via any other means without the permission of the publisher is illegal and punishable by law. Please purchase only authorized electronic editions, and do not participate in or encourage electronic piracy of copyrighted materials. Your support of the author's and publisher's rights is appreciated. Karma, it's everywhere.

PREFACE

The author, Count Luigi Ferdinando Marsigli (1658-1730), was an Italian soldier and scientific writer, who was born at Bologna on 10 July 1658. After scientific studies in his native city he travelled through Turkey collecting data on the military organization of the Ottoman Empire and other subjects. He then entered the service of Emperor Leopold in 1682. The next year Austria was invaded, and Vienna was besieged. Marsigli fought with distinction against the Turks, but he was wounded and captured by the Turks at the Rába River. He was subsequently sold into slavery and bought by a pasha who he met after the siege of Vienna. He was freed from slavery in 1684 and continued a military and literary career. This work is the result of what he had learned prior to the famous siege and what he observed first hand as a Turkish slave after the siege.

The original title of this work is Stato Militia dell' Imperior Ottomanno (The Hague: Pietro Gosse, 1732). Though this work was published long after that famous siege it is clearly a study of the Turkish army at that time. Originally it was published in both Italian and French. This is a translation of the French part of that original publication.

What is translated here is apparently a second volume, as on the title page it is identified as the "Seconde Partie." The first part is lost and its contents are not known though there are some references to it in the beginning of this work. That said, this part is clearly a study of the Turkish army and is quite complete in itself.

Notes on Translation

Because this work was published in 1732 it suffers from the pre-standardized French spellings and grammar. The spelling of Turkish words in this work were filtered through Marsigli's Italian and French. As a result, the Turkish words were, for the most part, difficult to translate into the modern spellings and, as a result, have been left as they were found.

This translation is as exact as I could make it, but the quality of the narrative was not very good, so I was forced to rewrite many sentences. That said, specific words and terminology has been kept as close to the original, despite the fact that it was written from the perspective of an 18th Century Christian speaking of Islamic issues at his time.

I have also maintained as much of the original graphics as the pagination would permit.

Sultan Mustapha II
(1695 - 1703)

Sultan Ahmet III
(1703 - 1730)

Preliminaries on the Military Operations of the Turks

The Military State of the Ottoman Empire
Part Two

The first part of this work was a translation of the *Canon-Name* necessary to bring the reader up to date on the constitution, the laws, and the regulations of the military state of the Ottoman Empire. I have, however, added from time-to-time some chapters that appeared appropriate to clarify what is contained in the *Canon-Name*; I do not believe that the reader will be completely satisfied, and I realize that I have not completed the task I have assigned to myself to give a detailed state of the forces of this empire. This work was prepared to supplement and clarify what was lacking in the *Canon-Name*; and which is necessarily linked; and I shall subsequently treat what was not mentioned in it. Thus I shall present in some manner the militias that are employed for the service of the Empire by detailing all the operations of the military art; and it is also necessary to make clarifications before entering into these details, I shall enclose them in some preliminary chapters, by which one will see how the Turks make war, without it being necessary to repeat them, so the reader shall find here that which is necessary to bring them up-to-date on their military operations. Finally, I will make a comparison of the first part and from the second, by which we can understand the few cases that we must realize about the Ottoman forces, whatever we believe about them, and how they appear to be so strong.

CHAPTER I
What is the Pay of the Janissaries and How are They Paid?

The last week of the quarter, chiefs and officers assemble in their Aga's house to hold a council. Each carries the rolls of his company; and of all these particular rolls, we make a double general state of them, to give them to the Treasurer, and to the *Bas-Chious*[1]. The latter examines how many purses are needed for an *oda*[2]; and then they are called forward. There are then as many purses as there are soldiers to receive them; they are removed from the heap[3] where they are given to them as the whole body of the infantry which is present; and, finally, they take to what is necessary for the payment of their companies to the captains. The next day, or the day after this general distribution, the captain orders the distribution known as the *Ulfe-Serghi*[4] taking this time to reduce the number of small coins, according to the exchange rate of Constantinople. On the day of this distribution, the lieutenant, the *vekil-carez,* the commissioner, and the ensign go to the captain's side: the latter checks his company's roll, drawn up on the original given to the Treasurer, and then calls his soldiers by name in this way ("Omer son of Muhammad, a native of Burse, who at the rate of 5 aspres per day must have 450 for his quarter.") telling him, "take it and go." If someone is found to be in debt to the *oda's* treasury, the commissioner takes care to hold his hand, and the debt is taken from his pay.

Since I have spoken of this *oda's* treasury chest, it is good to know that it is made of iron, and that each company has one in Constantinople in its quarter. Not only is the entire amount of a dead Janissaries' own property returned to them, which quite often amounts to 50,000 Risdales; but still the capital interest proceeds are 10%, and 12%. No one can dispose of the money in this box without the consent of the captain, lieutenant, commissioner, and ensign, who have a register of all those who enter and leave it; and nothing gets out of it without the captain's stamp, but it has to be used for tents, harnesses, and other similar equipment. However, this money is used to assist disabled and needy soldiers and for the ransom of slaves. In the latter case, they bring dancers to the neighborhood of the slave company that they have to buy, where, after a music concert and a ball, and after presenting the treasury chest to the assistants, soldiers are told that such a member of their company is a slave, for whom so much is demanded as a ransom. They are then exhorted to be charitable, what is called *Jesir-Duguni*, that is to say, "works piety for slaves", and then each one contributes to it, and throws what he intends to give into an urn covered with a piece of cloth, in which there is a hole made for the money.

---

[1] This is done in the manner practiced by the Christians. (Bektashi)
[2] Or company.
[3] All the money separated by purses is in the middle of the room, in a platoon.
[4] This distribution is made in several European states among the Christian powers on the Monday of every week.

CHAPTER II
The Reduction of the Janissaries.

I shall begin here by showing that the Turkish Militia is no longer the same today, as that which was once praised; and I will first examine the Janissary Corps.

The Grand Vizier Köprülü[5] realizing that the Kapikulu Militia was becoming more and more formidable to the Great Lord, which was constantly with him; and based the arrogance from its privileges, advised Sultan Mahomet IV to weaken it. He insinuated to him that it was not wrong to turn a blind eye to certain abuses which could serve to degrade it, representing to him that it was too dangerous to leave it in the heart of the Empire. This advice, which was followed by the Sultan, had all the effect that the Vizier expected; soon after, the chambers established for military exercises in each *oda* were no longer reviewed; and we saw the soldiers dispersed to several places, some abandoning themselves to laziness, and others leaving the painful exercise of arms to engage in commerce, or some lucrative profession.

This first cause of disorder brought about the change in the election of chiefs; without having any regard either for valor or for merit, favor and interest alone obtained all the jobs, several of which the Sultan had earlier passed to the power of the Vizier, who distributed them, as he sees fit. That of *Jenizer-Agasi* was of this number; it was a charge that the Great Lord had always had at his disposal, which he awarded to someone from among the Pages of the Seraglio, to make him independent from the Vizier. Ali was the first to benefit from this change; a simple gentleman serving in the Kapikulu Baths without talent and experience, but by the sole favor of his master, he saw himself raised to the dignity of *aga*; found himself commander of the militia, before knowing what the service was; and that at the time that the Empire was in a violent crisis, I mean after the battle of Nissa, where the Imperials gained such a complete victory, that the Sultan was forced to flee from Sophia. Ali stayed there, and the following year the Vizier created his *kaimekan*, or Lieutenant at the Gate, and after the battle of Slankamen where Köprülü was killed, he saw himself as Vizier, but had he barely received this first dignity of the Empire, than he lost it miserably. This innovation with regard to the election of chiefs made the job of a Janissary as dependent, and even contemptible, as it had previously been honorable and sought after. It was necessary to turn to recruits to complete this corps, and even to use prayers, and flattering promises to commit them to enter it.

I was in Constantinople in the winter after the Slankamen campaign, that is to say in 1692; and there I witnessed a *capy-cirmak,* or publication on the part of the Sultan in all the crossroads of the city. It promised to give the new Janissaries up to eight aspers a day, which is the highest pay that had ever been given to the old veterans, and he hoped for admission to the rank of *otturaks*, or dead-pay, unrestrained after the campaign, ratifying besides that the privilege, which one may well call abusive, to negotiate, and to exercise any kind of profession. To further engage in taking sides, the motif of religion was used, suggesting that it was in the service of God and the Prophet Muhammed to support this body. The day after this publication the *bas-chiaous* went to one of the large city squares, and put himself in the highest place, with the chiefs of the Janissaries arranged in a row on his right, and the lieutenants on the left, to be present at the enlistment of those who would join; but despite the promises of publication, I saw little eagerness. Those who presented themselves were asked for their name, that of their father, and of their fatherland; and the secretary that the *bas-chiaous* had brought was taking care of writing them down.

We then inquired into which company they wanted to serve, and we passed them there, without forgetting for their installation the bellows ceremony called *joldos*, which means "comrades." The company

---
[5] Köprülüzade Fazil Mustafa Pasha (1637 – 1691)

that had been chosen was then called, and the lieutenant received the new soldiers. This following the ancient custom of admitting neither Egyptians nor Arabs into this body, which was religiously observed, although these nations have the same law as the Turks. Then, new Janissaries were no sooner received, that, instead of applying themselves to the military exercises, they continued their ordinary professions, or began to embrace others; so it can be seen that this corps is few in number, and that however small it is, it has little experience in the profession of arms.

Janissaries at a banquet in 1720 (Topkai Palace). If the Sultan offered a banquet and the Janissaries refused it, it was a sign of displeasure that could lead to their revolt.

CHAPTER III
The Reduction of the Seratkuli Infantry.

The *Seratkuli* Infantry, intended for the place of the Janissaries, to form the border garrisons, where it originated and where it remains, is also reduced; but it was once looked at far below the *kapikulu*, but today it is the best militia of the Empire, because we were forced to send the Janissaries to garrison in the same borders, and that their bodies are greatly diminished. This one, as it was formerly, is also very much larger, even though it is almost extinct, particularly in Hungary, where it was maintained, as in its own country, in which it guarded all the fortresses, because part of the soldiers, either were born in this kingdom, or were inhabitants of it; and they died there. The Treasury was obliged to recruit this corps; in the absence of locals, we hired mountain men from Bosnia, Herzegovina and Albania, robust, ferocious people, capable of also using both swords and firearms. But it was by contracting with the chiefs, such as Mahomet Beg Regu, and paying 40, 50, and 60 risdales for each soldier that the chiefs delivered to the Army; and still we were forced to provide them with food on campaign. However, these soldiers were only required to serve three or four months during the summer, for which they had signed up; and they were then allowed to withdraw to their homes, pending a new agreement for the following campaign. This is how we replaced, in some way, the *Seratkuli* infantry, which, without these troops called the *Arnaut* numbered 15,000 to 20,000 men armed with long muskets, which would not have numbered 5,000 or 6,000 during the last campaigns of the Great Vienna War:

The Treasury, however, is still somewhat relieved in its excessive spending, not being obliged to dress the recruits, and not bothering about a uniform.

CHAPTER IV
The Reduction of the *Kapikulu* and *Toperakli* Cavalry.

The *Kapikulu* Cavalry Corps is made up of people drawn from the Seraglio, and that of the *Toprakli* Cavalry, which was reinforced during the conquests, by the extent of the *Beglerbas, Beglas, Ziamets,* and *Timars* are still considerably reduced. Obliged to spend more than their income, they no longer go into the field with the activity that Usciurs provide, or an abundant income. However, they did not lose so much strength for several years, only in their finance, since they were exhausted by the purchases of the harnesses, and by the expense of their own maintenance; and even that of horses.

A Siphai trooper in the 1670's.

CHAPTER V
Division of the Arms of the Turks.

The clarifications which were lacking in the *Canon-Name*, and which should, however, relate to it, are contained in the four preceding chapters. It, therefore, remains to speak of military operations; but, before I start, I have to give some more clarity on what concerns them, so that the reader can understand them more easily. It would lead into a kind of confusion to enclose them all in a single chapter, which I resolved to carefully avoid; thus, I shall give them in several, which nevertheless will, in a short time, make the reader fully aware of the operations which I must describe. I start with weapons.

The Turks use offensive and defensive weapons, which form the first division of their arms. The offensives are further subdivided into pointed weapons, cutting weapons and firearms; the latter still have a particular subdivision, which I will discuss below. Now let's see what their defenses are.

These weapons are of different kinds, I mean some are of iron, and of a particular or common wood, and others of iron and leather.

Those of iron are the two helmets called *zirin-culla*. The first marked "A" is completely round, and parallel to the skull, and the second, marked "B", stands on the head like a cone. They both have a third of the neck covered with an iron mesh; the first has both wings also of mesh, and the second has them of beaten iron. There is also the *zire*, or chain mail, marked "C", which they put like a shirt over a camisole stitched with cotton, and covered with canvas, on which are written certain superstitious words of the *Koran;* pretty much like what we call charms. Finally, there is a gauntlet, marked "D", called a "*colgiat*", which covers the arm up to the elbow; it defends the hand, and serves infinitely to ward off blows to the head.

Wood weapons are the shields, marked "E" and "F." They are most often made of fig, because this wood is light and is also a strong binder, that is suitable for countering thrusts and slashes. They are covered with skins, and very often of cotton ropes, which does not make them heavier.

The other shield marked "G" is of common wood. It is called a *buinduk*, and it is put on the neck of the horse. The Tartars use it a lot, especially when they fight with each other with their sabers, to try to protect their horses, which are their main strength; because as soon as they are dismounted, they are easy to defeat. These *buinduks* are very convenient in summer; they prevent the horse from turning its head to chase away the flies that so annoy the riders.

We see in Plate V the representation of all these kinds of weapons with the Turkish names they bear, so I won't say any more.

Plate I.

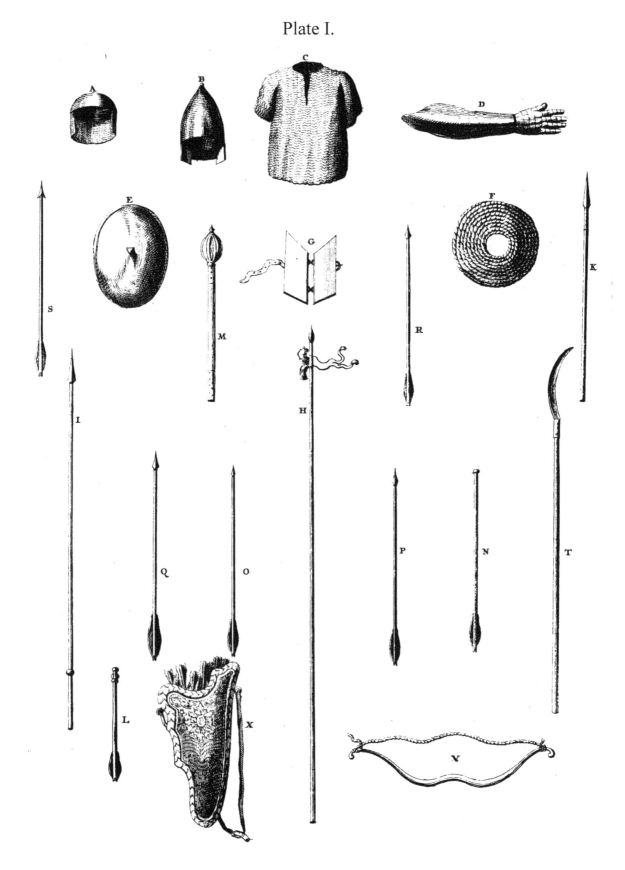

Explanation to Plate I

A. B. Two helmets called the *zirin-culla*. The first, marked A, is round and parallel to the skull. The second, marked B, is raised in a cone and both of them have a third covered with iron mail. The one has a mail neck guard and the other has the two wings of white iron.

C. The *zire*, or iron mail coat, as in Western Europe.

D. The *colgiac*, or bracelet with iron gauntlet.

E. F. The *calcal* or shield of fig wood. The first is doubled with fur on both sides; the second is covered with rope.

G. The *buinduk* formed with two blades, attached together as shown, which covers the horse's neck; the Tartars also use it.

H. The *karei-mesrac*, a type of lance used by the Asian Turks and the Kapikulu cavalry.

I. The *costaniza*, a type of lance used by the Seratkuli Cavalry. The ball prevents a counter blow.

K. The *kist* is a sort of javelin. The Agas' carry three of them in a quiver on the left of the saddle.

L. The *gerit* or *javelin*, of about two and a half feet long.

M. The *topeis* is a little *dard*, which is marked with the dignity of being carried on the left of the saddle.

N. The *oc* or arrow for exercises, which has a small wooden ball in place of a point.

O, P, Q & R. The *oclary*, or diverse types of arrows, be it by their point or length, which the Turks use.

S. The *tir-tartar* or arrows used by the Tartars. They are the longest of all.

T. The *terpan* or scythe.

U. The *ai*, or bow.

X. Quiver for carrying arrows.

CHAPTER VI
Weapons, Offensive and the First Type of Pointed Weapons.

There are three types of offensive weapons, being those with points, the cutting weapons, and firearms.

The first are lances, javelins, and arrows of different lengths.

The lances are long arms that are always held in the hand, but javelins are thrown and arrows, trimmed with feathers to better guide them, are fired with a bow. One sees representations of all sorts of these arms in Plate V, as well as those that are only used for exercises and in ceremonies.

The pointed arm called the *megge*, carried like a saber, and which is used in the same manner, is in the following plate. The Turkish names for all sorts of weapons are found with a short description of their usage.

CHAPTER VII
Edged Weapons

We see all the edged weapons carried by the Turks in wartime in Plate VI. They are all made to be used by hand and have it on the side of a sleeve in the form of an ax and on the other a point capable of piercing men, and horses. As I have said earlier, I placed in this plate, this type of weapon mounted like sabers, which are carried in a scabbard and are called *megge* in Turkish. It is a type of pointed weapon with which one pursues the enemy in order to stab them at a distance. It was heavily used by the Turks in Hungary, above all when out in groups; and they are attached to the saddle, so as not to forget their saber. This latter weapon is common to the infantry and to the cavalry. It is held on the side with a silken cord. We were especially careful that curved sabers could not embarrass anyone; and for that reason, we put the tip down. This shows that the way many of our Christian nations carry this kind of weapon is ridiculous; because it is suspended with two cords, like a balance.

The dagger is almost only used in parades by the Young Turks and a few Janissaries who carry it on the left side passed through the sash. They use it more in particular disputes and debates than in military functions; and they wound with the point not the edge, although it has a little sharpened edge.

This is all about the cutting weapons that the Turks use, among which, the four kinds of sabers, which they use on foot and on horseback, deserve to be considered for their lightness. In order not to stray from the goal that I have set out to detail everything concerning this military state, without passing any judgment on it, I pass over in silence, all that I could say about the use of the saber, which is the main weapon of this militia.

Plate II.

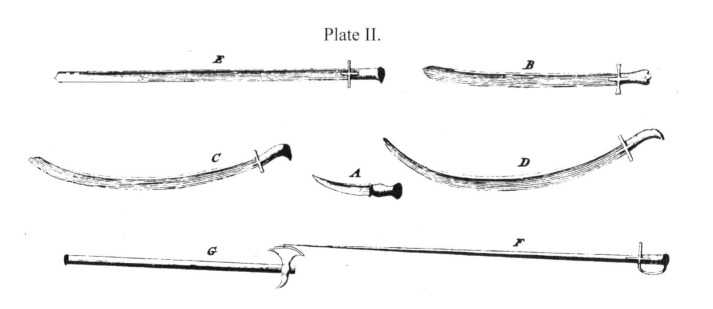

Explanation to Plate II

A. The *hangiar*, a type of dagger in the fashion of those of western Europe, which the Janissaries and the *Mignons* carry in Constantinople and which they pass through their sashes.
B. *Gadar'a* or saber, which is a bit curved, wide, and which is covered with iron.
C. The *clich* or sabre, used by the Turks.
D. A saber used by the Persians, which is more curved than that of the Turks, and is called the "*Agirm-clich*.
E. The straight *palas*, another type of saber.
F. The *megg* or skewer of a marked length which wounds with the point and which I put in the list of cutting weapons because of the blade and the manner in which it is used. The Hungarian frontier militia are armed with this.
G. The *tebet* is a type of axe which was carried on the saddle with the *topeis*, like the *palas* and the *gadar'a*.

CHAPTER VIII
Firearms and the First Portable Arms.

The pointed and the cutting defensive arms of which I have just spoken a few words are the proper weapons of the Tartars, and of the Turks. The usage of firearms, which I will presently speak of, came to them from the Christians, first by the wickedness of some individuals, whom, by avarice, or by vengeance, send them to them and then by capturing them in the wars they had with us in Europe. The siege of Candia [Heraklion, Crete] taught them better how they are served; and it was using these principles that they undertook the siege of Vienna. They started successively, during this war, to use many other kinds of weapons, which the Christians taught them to handle.

Firearms [cannon] quickly followed the invention of gunpowder and when the Turks begin to use gunpowder it was kept in iron containers, metal containers, and earthen containers. Various proportions were observed for the construction of these containers; and they were constructed such that a single man could carry and handle them, others which require the service of several persons, and others that were towed by horses, buffalo, or oxen; and finally, they enclosed it in underground hollows to blow up some work by its violence, which must be done on the spot.

The firearms of a Turkish soldier were very heavy matchlocks which fired balls of 6, 9, 12, 15 and 25 *dragmes*,[6] the musket in the style of the Spanish and a pistol which was smaller, and fired balls of 4, 6, and 8 *dragmes*.

The different caliber of these arms is the reason why the arsenal could not furnish balls. As a result, the Turks carried lead bars on ammunition carts to distribute to the soldiers, many of whom know the size of the bullets they need, and most of their weapons. So, for lack of caliber bullets, they cut lead pieces with an ax; and that serves them to load their weapons. Besides, it would be impossible for the arsenal to supply the multitude of weapons carried by the militia, if they themselves did not take care to arm themselves, and if the Porte did not receive those from Asia, which at instead of firearms only use stabbing weapons.

Long range muskets are too heavy to be carried in the field or to be fired without a fork, but they are carried everywhere by the Egyptian Janissaries, whom I have seen fire very accurately by putting the right foot back to help absorb the recoil.

Most of these muskets are inlaid with silver and some grains of coral in certain places. Each soldier has such ornaments and the Janissaries from Cairo particularly. They also embellish the wood with ivory, mother of pearl, and coral.

The Janissaries carry a pistol hung on their side, like a great part of the cavalry. One can see illustrations of all these weapons in Plate III.

---

[6] 1 dram is about 1/8 of an ounce or 1.77 grams

Plate III.

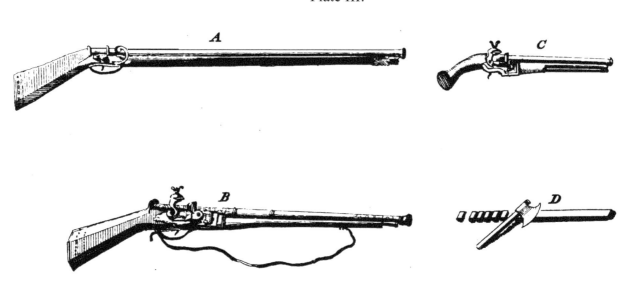

Explanation to Plate III.

A. Heavy Matchlock.
B. A flint-lock musket made in a form similar to those used in Spain.
C. A flint-lock pistol in the form of a musket.
D. Lead bar, which is cut up with an axe to make up for the lack of cast balls.

CHAPTER IX
Firearms That Must be Drawn;
Initially Cannons, Mortars, and Bombs.

    I now pass to the firearms of iron and metal, which must be drawn into battle by animals, as I have seen in sieges and in the battles. So as to not multiply the number of plates, I will put them all in two.

    First, it is necessary to see an iron cannon that fires 20-pound balls of stone, which, instead of handles has two iron rings below the chamber, through which one can pass ropes to attach it to some planks. It was thus at Buda[pest], where I saw the fortress from the Danube. I saw yet another one in the same way at Sighet; and I believe that these guns are of the invention of the Christians and not of the Turks, who only left them in the places where they found them; we see the figure in Plate IV.

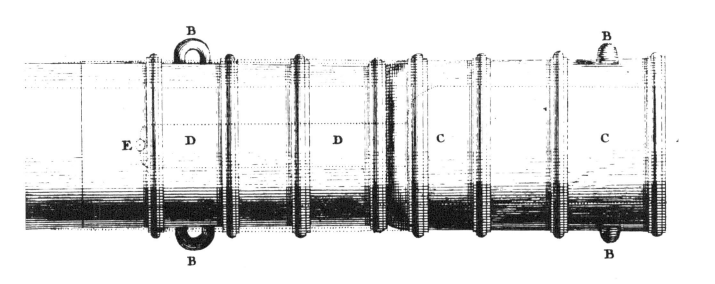

Explanation to Plate IV

A. Iron Cannon.
B.B.B.B. Four ears in the form of handles.
C.C. Mouth of the cannon where he stone shot is placed.
D. Powder chamber.
E. Touchhole.

The second plate shows the type of bronze cannons that the Turks have lost in fortresses and in battles; and here one sees a 12-pound cannon. The smallest I have seen come from the Constantinople Foundry, like the largest that fire 40-pound balls (Nuremberg pounds) and which was at Buda[pest], are all of the same form, with varying lengths and calibers. In the examination that I have made, I have noted that they were founded following the plan of Pierre Sardi, as well as an Italian, during the siege of Candia [Heraklion, Crete], whom both had placed the foundry in order; and I found in Constantinople a book on Sardi's artillery translated into Turkish.

The Turks do not put coats of arms on their cannon as is the practice in Europe; but a bit above the handles are verses from the *Koran* and praises of the reigning sultan in Turkish characters.

They conserve with great care the pieces of artillery that they find in conquered Christian fortifications, because they surpass those of the Turks in their beauty. In contrast, we recast captured Turkish cannon so as to make them in our style. Reports say that large quantities of the cannon that the Turks have lost were recast in the Vienna Arsenal to make new ones.

I have judged it necessary to present in Plate IX the carriages of the Turkish cannon and above all those of the heaviest cannon, as they are most curious and we have profited on occasion, especially with regards to the very different Turkish wheels, not having the practice of turning large wheels with so many spokes as are done in Western Europe. The wheel, which is attached to the carriage, is made from several planks tied together as we can see, and the one which is separated from it, and which is in the shape of a barrel, is all in one piece, shod with iron in the middle and at both ends. The axles are of solid iron, and the figure and the proportion are engraved in the same plank. I saw in the time that I was in the Turkish army, that the artillery thus mounted was hardly fired; and having asked them why they used such wheels, they replied, that it was so as not to be obliged to raise the batteries so high. Indeed, this use would not be harmful to us in fortresses.

Plate V

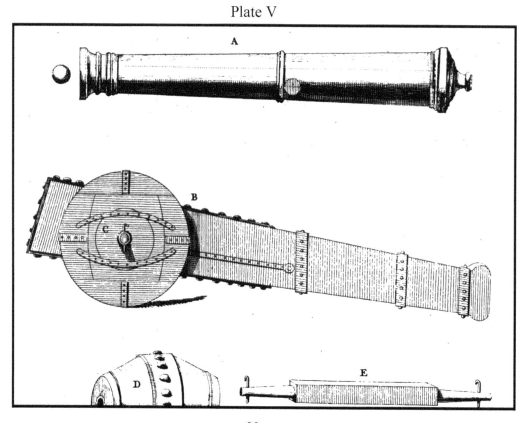

Explanation to Plate V.

A. 12-pound cannon intended to fire balls.
B. Carriage made and fitted with iron by the Turks.
C. Wheel made of several planks attached and banded in the Turkish manner.
D. Wheel hub in the form of a barrel.
E. Iron Axle.

After the capture of Buda, the Turks created a new type of carriage. The Grand Vizier Suleiman-Pasha wishing to relieve Segedin was defeated by General Veterani and left in the hands of the Imperials a number of 8-pounder cannons mounted on four-wheel carriages and the barrel rested on two iron forks, as one sees in Plate VI.

Plate VI

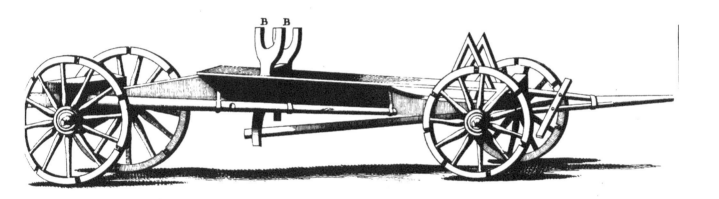

Explanation to Plate VI.

A. Gun Carriage.
B.B. Forks on which the handles of the cannon are supported.

After the battle of Patakin, in 1690, which the Imperials won, the Turks placed two 3-pounder cannons on the saddles of many camels and a Turkish gunner was mounted behind them. But having recognized their folly and seeing that these animals were not sufficiently fast, they cut their legs without taking to remove the artillery pieces, which were captured by the Imperial troops. A similar effort greatly entertained us, but we only saw them at a distance. Plate VII shows this plan.

Explanation to Plate VII.

A. Cannon which had another on the other side.
B. Iron fork on which the cannon rests
C. Iron armor on which the fork is attached.
D. Turkish gunner.
E. Strap with which the gunner raises or lowers the gun.

The Turks also use bronze mortars to firebombs and stones. One can see a representation of them in Plate XII with their proportions; they are like those found in the fortresses they lost.

Plate VIII

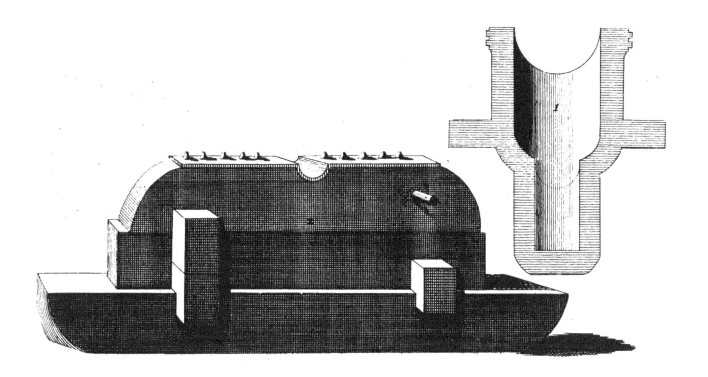

Explanation to Plate VIII

I. *Van Cumbarasy*, or bomb mortar.
II. *Van Cundac*, or mortar carriage.

The Christians taught them how to bombard. In recent times a bombardment officer of the Serene Republic of Venice saved himself at Negroponte and then became a Turk and the General of the Bombardiers of the Porte. He was given a great salary and perfected his art. One can see in the same plate the form of the mortar carriage.

Their bombs are of various sizes, but roughly thrown; however, they had enough effect, as at Belgrade, when they set fire to the gunpowder magazine.

CHAPTER X.
Artifice Fire for Illumination and Setting Fires

The artifice fire of the Turks, the most part of which consists of gunpowder, appears to me to be very simple and are only employed to illuminate or to burn.

Plate XIII shows a *tuyau* at the end of an iron tipped pike, and the use this particular device on ships. One can see, after this figure, a Tartar arrow, which has the arrowhead surrounded by small bits of wood and straw, which are lit by a sulfur wick. They fire this arrow with a bow against the roofs of houses, especially in Hungary, to set fire to those which the pike, of which I will speak later, cannot reach.

The third figure represents an arrow, which I have seen the Turks use, at the time when I was a slave, during their invasion of Austria. It is a small ball of combustible material in the form that you can see, and they fire it against houses. One can also see a pole at the end of which is straw filled with sulfur wicks, which the Tartars threw at houses to set them on fire during the invasion of Austria (1683). There are two other poles that serve to light the army by means of fires on their ends. The first is an iron basket filled with straw and tar, which is planted in several places in the camp so that everyone can see the baggage being loaded, and the horses harnessed. At the end of the second there is a small canvas lantern with a lighted candle, which is carried on the shoulders. We always saw a large quantity of them, when the army is on the march during the night, to light the way, and even so that the guides, who carry them can warn about bridges, ditches, and anything that could delay the march.

I saw the Turks use three fires during the siege of their fortresses. The first consists of pans of tar attached to the end of a pike, which they place outside their walls and in which they place burning tar. The second place they illuminate in several places is the covered way and the ditch, with small fires of dry wood mixed with sulfur and tar to permit firing to be easier. Finally, they fire balls of combustible material to illuminate places. I have seen three types of fire in 1693, during the siege of Belgrade, when they attacked the counterscarpe during the night.

Finally, the Turks have the custom of placing gunpowder in bags of goat skin, which they hold in the form of small sacks of a size that a single man can handle them, like grenades, and they throw them into the breach during an assault. They used them during the second siege of Buda[pest] and the garrison was greatly discommoded.

Plate IX.

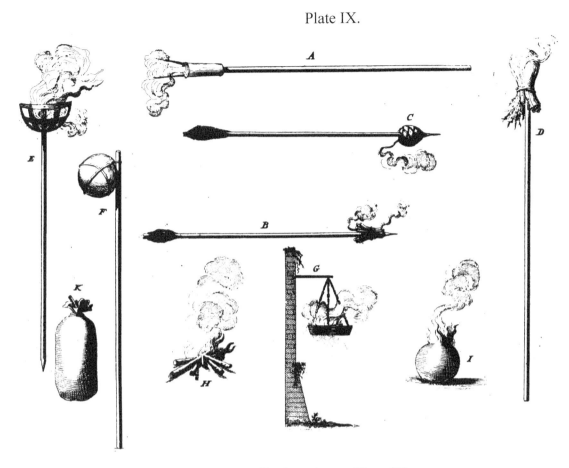

Explanation to Plate IX.

A. *Tuyau* at the end of a pike, with an iron point to be driven into the wood so that the fire can spread.
B. Tartar arrow, which has part of the point surrounded with small bits of wood and straw, which is lit with a sulfur wick.
C. Tartar arrow with a small ball of combustible material, which is thrown against houses.
D. Pole on the end of which there is a bundle of straw mixed with sulfur matches, which the Tartars use to burn houses.
E. Iron grill with tar and straw, at the end of a pole, which is plated in several places around the camp so one can see while loading the baggage.
F. Canvas lantern at the end of a pole, where a lighted candle is placed. It is carried on the shoulder to illuminate the way at night.
G. Iron pan filled with tar and attached to a pike, which is placed outside the walls of a fortress.
H. Pile of dry wood with a bit of sulfur and tar to illuminate, which is placed in several locations in the covered way and dry ditches.
I. Ball of combustible material to illuminate things.
K. Bag of goat skin in which one places gunpowder, which is tied like a small sack to serve in the manner mentioned above.

CHAPTER XI.
Mines

I will finish this part which looks at the effect of the fire by the Turks by the demonstration of the art of making mines, in which they excel. These mines are pits that we invented so that the powder contained either in the ground, or in a wall has the strength to have the effects that we know. We use mines in the places we want to force, instead of the other devices in which we put the powder that always follows an army.

The Turks learned the art of mining during the long siege of Candie [Heraklion, Crete], by the skill of quantity of workers whom they have for the mines dispersed throughout the Empire, and even of some Armenian masons. The Porte, as it has already been said, had the custom of distinguishing them by privileges to which it adds very high pay. I had occasion, being in Constantinople, to discuss this with certain Armenian directors of the mines, who even teach the art. They gave the following answers to several questions I gave them:

That, to measure the distance from a wall that we wanted to destroy, we used a capable and enterprising miner, who, with a stone attached to a string, went at night to the place where we had resolved during the day to make the first opening of the gallery. Whether this miner crawled on the ground or stayed at the end and threw this stone to the foot of the wall; and then cutting the rest of the rope, he dragged the rest into the neighboring entrenchment, where he measured it, and calculated the distance that the gallery of the mine must have, as we can see in Plate XIV.

That, to direct the gallery, one rarely used a compass; but we used sights in a semicircular frame, shown by Figure B-B., called *lagum tabiascy* (the first word means mine, & the second battery of muskets) with bullets along the gallery. That at the beginning as in the middle, we dropped a weight every time, that we needed to see if the gallery ended at the ordered point, by putting a lighted candle at the end.

That, the shape of the gallery was round in the upper part, like Figure C, the gate; and that it was a little higher than half the size of a man, because we dug with our legs crossed. That it was kept as close as possible, so that small baskets of dirt could be pulled out with ropes to empty it. The workman also told me that it was very inconvenient for them to load the mine in such a narrow gallery; but, on the other hand, that they still hoped for success, because they did not have such a large opening to fill up with the bags of earth and wool.

In order to ventilate the gallery, we pierce the vault with an auger, obliquely all around, as we can see by the Figure D.

The shape of the mine chamber that the Turks call "*asna*," or "treasure", is in a semicircle, and resembles that of the mine chamber which one sees in Figure E.

That, to load the mine, they spread a canvas on the very earth of the mine chamber, E, on which they pour out the powder without pressing it. Then they put a wooden grill over the same width of the furnace, as Figure F, called "*asna-agag*," that is to say "treasure wood."

To close the mouth of the mine chamber, we used two pieces of wood called "*oluk*," of the same shape as seen in Figure G, of which the one below had a hole, H, to pass the sausage[7] called "*fetil*," full of combustible material, which we placed as in Figure E, and the letters. I. I. I. We fill the gallery with woolen and earthen bags, and we interlace them six by six feet long with beams placed on each side of the gallery, which we call "*mertek*," as in Figure L which is a piece of gallery filled in this way.

---
[7] Translator: The "sausage" is a tube of gunpowder that serves as a fuse.

All the preceding figures contribute to forming a Turkish in its state by fact, where the fire is carried to Point M by means of the aforementioned sausage full of gunpowder. All of Figure N.N., shows everything that forms a perfect mine, as the Turks do it, and which they call "*lagumce*" which means "mine."

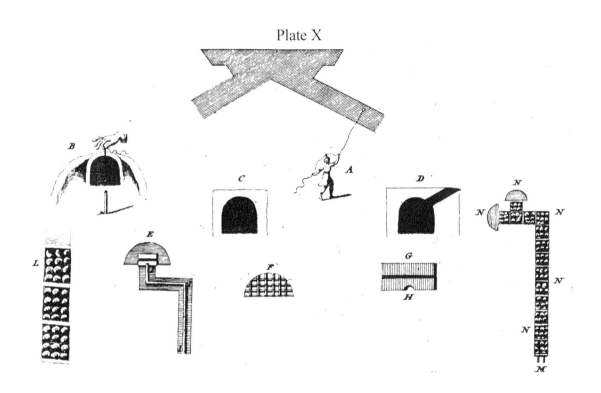

Plate X

Explanation of Plate X.

A. Miner, who throws a stone attached to a cord to the foot of a wall to measure the distance and then to be able to calculate the length of the gallery needed for the mine.
B. Semicircular frame, called the "*lagum-taniascy*", where one makes marks with bullets to serve as a guide the length of the gallery and at the beginning of which, in the middle, one hangs a plum bob.
C. Form of the Turkish gallery is round, towards the upper part.
D. Drill with which one drills an oblique in the roof of the gallery from place to place to ventilate it.
E. Mine chamber, called the "*asna*" or "powder treasure."
F. Grill of wood called the "asna-agag." It also called the "treasure wood."
G. Two pieces of wood called the "*uluk,*" used to close the mouth of the mine chamber.
H. Hole in the lower part through which the sausage (fuse), called the "*fetil*," is passed the length of the gallery, as shown in figure E, by letters I, I, I.
L. Part of a gallery filled with bags filled with dirt.
M. Place where the sausage is ignited.
N. Perfect mine in the Turkish manner, called the "*lagum.*"

CHAPTER XII.
Horses of the Turkish Cavalry

Cavalry is a considerable part of the Turkish army. Among the Turks it is more numerous than the infantry, because their land abounds in horses. It is by means of their cavalry that they have rendered themselves masters of Anatolia. They naturally like to ride their horses and as a prince is much more powerful when he has a greater number of good ones, I thought it necessary to speak of those of the Ottoman cavalry, in a particular chapter, after the description of their arms.

The Turks are generally, according to their taste, the number of their horses and their efforts increase the number of their horses, undertake with care the good *haras*. They spare them extremely and do not employ them like Europeans, to hall wagons, carriages or as pack animals. No matter what their age, they prefer to ride their horses, outside of the militia; and also, if age prevents them from riding, they prefer to stay at home, to riding in a carriage, a vehicle that is reserved for women, even though they rarely travel. These carriages are only drawn by to horses.

The nature of their horses varies according to the provinces and kingdoms of the Empire from which they are drawn. Those from Europe are generally robust, have a heavy head, and are not very fast. In contrast, those from Asia have a delicate nature and limbs and are very proper for raiding. Between those from these two parts of the world, there are differences from province to province, as I have said.

In Europe, those from Hungary are of a good height, but those from Transylvania are better for walking and have good chests and croups. We have in this province the convenience of having mares from Moldavia, which borders there; which produces excellent horses for walking, and are easy to train, which have great rumps and chests, and the rather large legs; and which are very resistant to fatigue. We considered them the best in the army, as well as the Polish horses. In Wallachia they are generally very rough[8], and prone to flinching, and their size is hardly above mediocre.

In the Provinces of Budgiack, and of Ozacov, inhabited by the Tartars dependent on the Kam of Crimea, one finds horses there, which have large heads, heavy indeed, and of a mediocre height; but tireless, and need little nourishment. They also eat all kinds of grass, good or bad, green or dry. The Tartars eat the flesh of these horses themselves, which they find very delicate, and drink the milk of the mares. These animals fear neither cold nor heat, and always trot. There are no rivers or marshes that stop them, and they swim with the rider naked, as I will say below. They are raised in the marshes of Budgiack and around the Danube, Nister, Borissene, and other rivers that water Crimea, that they continually cross from morning until evening, to shorten the path, hardly caring about bridges.

In the land of Dobra, which is this vast plain between Mount Hemus, the Danube, the Jantra, and the Black Sea, which is Lower Bulgaria, there come quite coarse horses, but of a large size. They are highly regarded in Turkey; and there is no officer of the Porte, who must go on horseback to the Divan, who does not try to have a Turkmenian horse to ride, looking more for height than finesse in this ceremony, since the horses are richly caparisoned, and have gilded silver harnesses.

Bosnia, Serbia, and Albania, and the landlocked provinces in the mountains, have very small horses, that are passably built and not very delicate.

Greece, and Thrace provide horses in the vicinity of Constantinople, which are rather bastards of the others which leave Asia, and Europe. I have seen all kinds, instead of one particular, as in all the other

---

[8]Translator: The word "grossier" is used and can mean "rough" or "stupid." The translation of the Italian suggests that "rough" is the proper translation.

parts of the Empire.

Asia produces horses quite different from those of Europe, for their size, their naturalness, and the food they eat. The Turks of this part of the world have more passion for breeding horses, and take much more pleasure in it than Europeans, who by the means of the mares, and stallions, have infinitely improved their horse stock. This passion can only be highly commended; these animals deserve to be sought; and nature has greatly benefited them. They are all generally well made with the exception of those of Turkmenia, the first homeland of the Turks, as I have said, where they are tall and coarse, and are only esteemed at the Court for parades.

The beauty, and the finesse of the horses increases as one advances towards Syria, and as one passes the Euphrates to enter Persia, and in Arabia. Generally speaking, the horses of these countries have very fine nostrils, and large eyes; and if they have a broad chest, they have a narrow rump; on the contrary if they have a wide rump, they have a narrow chest; and these two parts of the body are rarely found equal in size. They have a gut as much as necessary, with very fine skin, as well as hair; and we even see their blood running under the skin, especially at the head which is very delicate. That of the other horses, which passes for well made, is too big in comparison with these. Their manes are very fine, and very clear; we leave them open to show their beauty in the process. Their tails are long and loose. Their hooves are very strong; but such fine horses are badly trained. Firstly, because they are only ridden at five years of age, the Turks wanting the horse's body to have all its strength, which does it wrong, since it then has stiff legs. This natural defect prevents them from handling well; and they are neither trotted nor galloped, this being not in use among the Turks; but they immediately put them on the brisk step, then trot them with their stiff legs. In the race they never stop without passing the goal and turning their heads. These bad habits come only from lack of discipline, since the horses are, moreover, very docile, and they lose these faults, as soon as they have been with us for some time, although already old. They are quite delicate in their naturalness, unable to suffer from cold or humidity, and that is why they are always covered in the stables, where the Turks even keep a fire, making a trench for their manure, so that it dries, to make litter. They are even less uncovered in the countryside, and we have different covers, depending on the degree of cold or hot. I remember that at the end of August, during the siege of Vienna, the Asian horses began to perish because of the coolness of the nights; and indeed, upon returning from the Hungarian campaigns, they are almost always ruined. They feel the fire, and go there only with difficulty, which is very inconvenient in action, because they are not easily handled.

Their regular food is chopped straw, oats and barley; and their ration weighed six *ockes*.[9] We split it in two; and give them half in the morning, and the other half in the evening. That of the Sultan's horses goes up to eight *ockes*, and one more of hulled barley. If in the field they are given other grains, hay, or worse, grass, they perish, either because they lose weight, or they begin to cough, or finally they become winded.

We must except the horses of Turkmenistan who are not easy to feed because of the delicate hay of Armenia which they usually eat. To keep them cold, they are kept in underground stables, where they have water near the trough, so that they can drink whenever they are thirsty.

I was curious to see in Constantinople the Sultan's stables in which I found all along a platform raised by the width of a palm, and wide the whole length of the largest horse, where one spreads the night on a big blanket of felt, on which the horse lies down, and which should not be necessary. There is then on each side a tub to put the manure that the grooms take care to deposit outside, always keeping the stables clean. All these horses were covered and had a mark on their left thigh.

All those who have the convenience of having grooms prefer Arabs to do that work as they excel in

---
[9] Translator: The *okka* weighs 1.282 kg (2.83 lbs)

this profession. They take two hours whole to braid a horse, they rub the skin with their hands, and remove the smallest hair that is longer than the others. They polish it with various felts, and even use soap. They often dye the mane and the tail red of the white horses, with equine dye, which is brought from Cairo in powder to paint the hands, the feet, and even the heels of the women who have this whimsical taste.

Everywhere I have said about these horses, we can judge how little they are worth outside their country, how much autumn and winter inconvenience them in Europe, how expensive they are, and how they do not survive long.

Finally, there is no land where horses are so expensive, only on the borders of pious Arabia, and mainly when they are of a famous breed. If they have an authentic genealogy of at least six generations, and the seller gives it to the buyer, we will sometimes pay 2,000 Risdales for a horse. I have a treatise on the horses from Persia, Arabia, and Syria translated from the Turkish, which deserves to be made public, and which will please the curious.

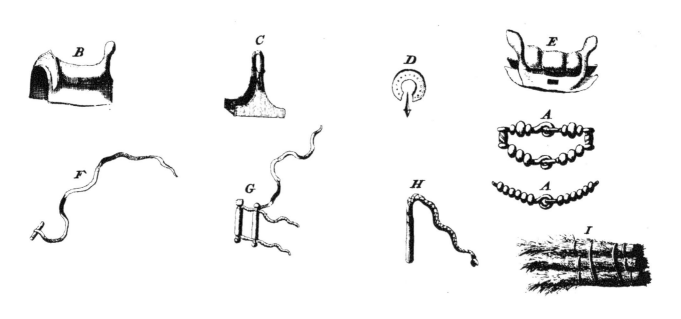

Plate XI.

Explanation to Plate XI.

A. The bit, called the *"legem."*
B. The saddle, called the *"eger."*
C. Stirrup, called *"ussengy,"* whose sole is very large and is made of heavy metal.
D. Horseshoe, called *"at-naali,"* very thin with nails with a diamond point.
E. Light saddle used by the Tartars.
F. Reins of leather with various holes to permit the passage of a wooden button when they are attached to the chain.
G. Two sticks that serve as a bridle.
H. Whip.
I. Flying jumper, called a *"saidan-sal"*, formed from a bundle of reeds or other swamp grass which they attach to the tail of the horse to break it of bad habits.

CHAPTER XIII.
Turkish and Tartar Harnesses.

We must necessarily speak of harnesses, after having mentioned horses. I divide them into those used by the Turks and those used by the Tartars.

Those of the Turks include the bit called a *"legem,"* as we see it in Plate XV, marked with the letter A. The saddle is bare and without any ornament of the form that we see in Figure B, called an *"eger."* The stirrups are called *"us-segny."* They have a wide base on which to place the foot that is made of heavy metal, which beat the sides of the horse on both sides; they are made as shown in Figure C. Iron horseshoes cover the hooves more than those of Europe; they are very thin and very light and have diamond-tipped nails. We see the representation of them in Figure D. They are called " *at nalı*," in Turkish, that is to say "horseshoes."

The Tartars have a very light saddle as seen in Figure E and use their coats or some bed cover for cushions, as it appears in the same plate. While I was a slave, I saw several during the great incursion into Austria who were on horseback, and who had no brake, but only leather reins pierced in several places to pass a wooden button, when they attached the curb; and by this form of bridle marked F, they led him. But as it has no particular name, I will not name it here. They still use two sticks marked G, as a bridle, which they attach them to the horse's nose; and they also use it to lead their horses, and to cut his hooves with a red-hot iron; because they leave them bare; this iron is named *"burun-salik."* The whip with the short handle, marked H, is highly esteemed by the Tartars; and it is with reason, since it does all their good, because by dint of spanking their horses, they arrive in the places where they hope to take slaves. They call it *"can gy."* We also see the representation of their flying saddletrees, made of bundles of reeds, and other marshy grasses. They call it *"sas-dan-sal"*, and put it over their old clothes, their bow, the arrows, and the saber, to keep them dry, when they are forced to swim. They have similar bundles which they attach to the shoulders of poor slaves, when they force them to cross streams by making them hold both hands on the tail of their horses. I myself was obliged to do this at the four passages of the canals that form Lake Neisiden, from which the Rammiz River takes its source, as we see in Plate XVI, and even without the help of this fascine [bundle of reeds], notwithstanding the great wounds I had. These passages were truly an object worthy of pity, to see the misery of the Christians, since the one who released the horse's tail, infallibly drowned, and if anyone refused to pass thus, there were Tartars on the banks with the naked saber ready to cut off his head.

Finally, the whip, the skill of the Tartars, and their habit of crossing rivers as I said are to be noted, since only one lying in a shirt on the back of his horse with his whistle, and his whip can make 20 horses and other cattle cross a river, which we should fear more than their sabers. To make the way in which the Tartars pass streams more intelligible, I give a representation of it in Plate XII, with all its parts.

Plate XII.

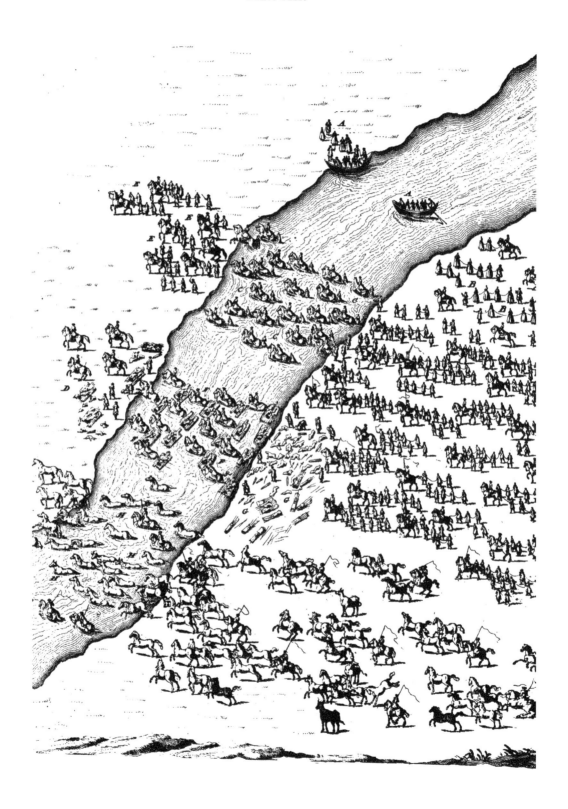

Luigi Marsigli

Crossing a River by Swimming

The Tartars crossing the canal between Lake Naiasiller and Rhebao Island, where the author found himself among the slaves. One can see in this representation the barbaric manner with which the Turks carry their booty, be it cattle, slaves, or horses. They cross the water by swimming and keep their weapons dry.

The Crossing is Made in Four Locations

The first crossing location was in two fishing boats marked A.A., which were found on the shore, and which were loaded with women and children; and on the other side there are other women who were to be embarked under the guard of some Tartars. This is marked B.B.

The second crossing location is that marked C.C., where there are some Tartars, each leading a slave who holds on to the tail of the horse, with their legs bound. The author crossed the canal in this manner. Each Tartar is in his shirt whistling and crying on the shore marked D, where there are other slaves waiting to cross. On the other side, E, the Tartars remount their slaves and lead off the poor, chained slaves.

The third crossing, marked F, is that of the Tartars, who have a bundle of reeds tied to the tail of their horses, on which they place their weapons and clothing, which they keep dry and prevent from sinking while the horses swim the canal.

There are some more of these bundles of reeds on the side marked G.G. for those who need them.

The fourth crossing is marked H.H. and is that of the cattle and horses, where some tartars also swim, with their whips in their hands, marked I.I. and with cries and whistling, chasing their animals across the canal, which is wider and deeper here.

The Tartars swim on their horses without saddle, stretched out on their backs or rumps, holding onto the mane and sometimes elsewhere.

CHAPTER XIV.
Standards and Flags

It is the standard practice of all the armies formed of several small corps that each corps be guided by a flag, which is in sight of each soldier. The Turks do the same; and in addition, on ceremonial days, when approaching battle and within sight of the enemy and tributaries, they augment the number of their flags, believing that they will inspire more terror in the enemy and raise the courage of their tributaries. I shall report, as evidence of this, what I have seen during the siege of Vienna, while a slave in their army. Two days before, there were a few small wagons, some rustic, that brought food; there were only one or two red cloth banners. They then put them on the horse of cattle and buffalo and attached along the length of their cannon three or four with ropes. All the cavaliers who were armed with lances, which I mentioned in that chapter on the offensive stabbing arms, also had bits of red silk banners such as those carried by the Kapikulu Sipahi. This was at the express order of the Grand Vizier, who thought these "weathercocks" would frighten the garrison. In addition, at a distance would inform the viewer who the troops were, and perhaps those, who had climbed the bell towers of Vienna that the Turkish army was larger than it was.

These flags must be divided into these small banners at the end of a lance carried by the Kapikulu Cavalry as we see on Plate XVII, and into those of the Janissaries, the Timar Cavalry, and bombardiers which are in Triangles, and of different color, with a two bladed saber, and cannoneers, with the figure of a cannon and a ball, the pashas, and the viziers have a fairly large standard and almost uniform, at the end of which is a ball of golden copper; it is all filled with gold embroidery that is made in the Isle of Chios.

The noblest standard is the hand-made ponytail. They join several together, dye them red, and then make a head with small horsehair cords that fall on the tail for greater ornamentation, mixing white and black, and the whole is surmounted by a large ball of gilded copper, in the costume of the Tartars, which the Turks kept to distinguish the commanders. That of a small department called "*beg*" has one; and that of a province which bears the name of a pasha has two. The *belerbegs* who have the rank of vizier and who reside in capital cities of the kingdoms or conquests, have three; the Grand Vizier five; and when the Sultan goes on the campaign, he has seven.

It remains to give the description of the Standard of Mohammed that the Sultan allows to leave the Seraglio and be carried into the field with the main army; but as I never saw it deployed on the march, halfway through camp in the tent of the treasury, I did not want to assume the relationship. In fact, I will only say that in so many defeats that they suffered in Hungary, they always found a way to save it, because they always sent it in front with a strong escort. Those who escorted it after the battle of Slankamen were largely rewarded, because they said that by a miracle of their false prophet, he had become invisible when passing through the Imperial Cavalry.

Plate XIII.
Flags and Standards

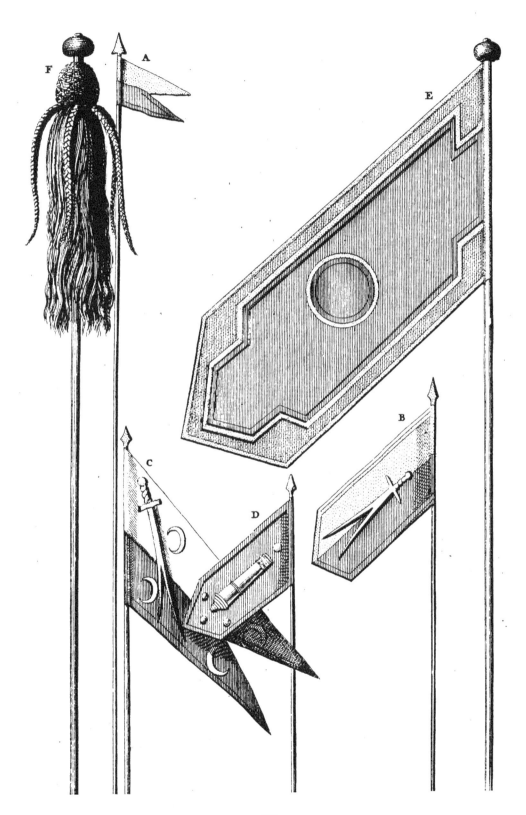

Explanation to Plate XIII.

A. Small banner at the end of a lance carried by the Kapikulu Cavalry.
B. Flag of the Janissaries.
C. Standard of the Toprakli Cavalry with two bladed saber.
D. Flag of the cannoneers bearing a cannon.
E. The standard of the pashas and viziers with a gilded copper ball on top and it is edged with gold.
F. Horse tail made with the manes of several horses joined together, dyed red, and tied together with small cords to form a head.

CHAPTER XV.
Instruments of the Army's Musicians

The Turks sound and percussion instruments used in their armies, are made according to different forms, which I give in the Plate XVIII., and which, with the exception of one, are used for the pomp of a ceremony, rather than for military exercise.

For percussion instruments they have two kinds of drums, and an instrument composed of two metal dishes.

Their sound instruments are a curved metal trumpet, and a wooden torch.

The bass drum called a "*daul*," is three feet high; the drums are carried on horseback with a collar covered with red cloth; and the drummers strike on the upper part with a large stick of boxwood made in the manner shown on the plate, and on the lower with a small wand, striking alternately with each with great skill, and gravity, which is very pleasant. This is the only instrument which, in addition to the splendor of the pasha, is used for military exercises, because one beats these large drums, when the army is close to that of the enemy, all around the camp, to keep the guards awake, the drummers shouting "*Jegder alla*," that is, "God is great!"

The two small drums, or timpani, are marks of honor for the pashas' families, and serve as a signal for marching; they fit very well into the music concert, and they are called "*sadar nagara*." The three-tailed pashas have two timpani, and the timpani's are on each side of the saddle, and they are beaten as at home.

There enters into this concert another kind of instrument which is called "*zil*." It is a type of cymbal and consists of two metal disks with depressions in them, thin and hollow, on the convex side of which there is a ring, through which one passes two or three fingers. They are played by striking them one against the other, and the sound is silvery, and very pleasant. The three-tailed pashas have two men who play this instrument.

There are two sound instruments; and they differ as much in the way they are played, as in the material of which they are composed. The first is the trumpet: it is quite long, and made of the same metal as ours, as we can see by the figure. It is called a "*bori*." It is principally played on horseback and the pashas with three tails have seven.

The second is of wood; it is a kind of bagpipe composed of five pipes, as we can see by the figure. It is called a "*zurnader*. Whoever plays it is on horseback, and the three-tailed pashas have five.

The different sounds of all these instruments would be hard on the ear if they were not corrected by that of the great drum; but, when they are all together, the concert is quite pleasant.

Plate XIV.

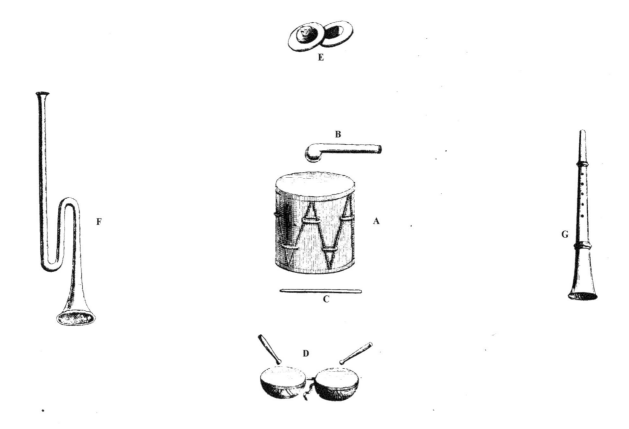

Explanation to Plate XIV.

A. Drum called the "*daul.*"
B. Large wooden stick with which the drum is struck on the top.
C. Small Stick with which the bottom of the drum is struck.
D. Small drums called the "*sardar-nagara.*"
E. The "*zil.*"
F. Trumpet or "*bori.*"
G. The "*zurnader.*"

CHAPTER XVI.
Tents

Upon the defeat of the Turks before Vienna the Imperials won many great victories over them and captured their camps. These victories always cost them the tents of the first viziers, the pashas, the officers and the soldiers. It was easy for the Imperials to judge if these tents were superior to theirs; be it for their material, for their shape, and the diverse proportions that the Turks observed in them; or for their functionality; because they were impenetrable to rain, sun, wind, and other injuries; be it finally for the sumptuousness and the beauty they presented, when they were set up in their camp. They were all made of cotton, which made them very heavy, though they were sufficiently low, because the Turks only sit on tiles, or carpets lying on the floor, where Europeans use benches. To overcome this defect, we chose German canvases that are much lighter, and suitable for easier erection. We match the different proportions; tents were made to camp, and easy to pitch, which was continued later, during the war which lasted for up to seven months on the desert plains of Hungary. Without this reform in the figure, and the material of the tents, after the rout of the Turks at Vienna the Imperial army would have been very embarrassed by so many thousands of tents that it had taken from the Turks, and especially if the slaves had not learned how to erect them.

In my opinion, this is what the Turks have taught us that is most useful. They themselves learned it from the Tartars, their ancestors, who always tried to refine the method of camping in tents, as has already been reported, to satisfy their need for luxury and their softness. Turks who possess great wealth do not seek less amenities, and pomp in their camps. After the so many successive conquests that they had made, one never saw among them more magnificence than in their camp in front of Vienna; and even, we can say that the luxury we saw there was there in its last phase.

They use flag tents, attached to a pole to support them, which have only one cover. They have them with two stakes, and also with a simple cover; and the general and subordinate officers as well as the pashas indifferently have a double cover, although their tent is only supported by a single pole. The shape of these tents is hexagonal, and the edges fall perpendicularly from the knot which supports the tent in the middle, which makes it the crown, and which is supported by ropes. These kinds of tents are used for sleeping comfortably in the late fall, because it is lined with a good tick of camel hair. They also have open tents to close the latrines. Throughout the Turkish army, there is only a single stake tent with a single dome, without an edge, which is the first of all that we set up in the camp, and which served as a guide to the master quarters of all the corps to intimidate.

It is in this those criminals and slaves are killed; and we call it a "*lailac*." The pashas have a sort of tent for the march, which looks rather like a parasol; it is used for coffee or a snack. This tent, which is open from the front, has only one pole on each side; and is supported by four ropes. The Grand Vizier has a canvas screen, high enough so that one cannot see in the enclosure of his tents; and this guarantees him from the inconvenience caused by men and horses hitting his tents, especially at night. Several other first-order pashas also have these kinds of screens; but only half the height of a man; which sufficiently defends them from the above inconvenience; it would be disrespectful to equal theirs with that of the Grand Vizier.

We should now speak of the tents used by the sultans, and principally those of Mahomet IV, which are all very convenient, and suitable for the pomp and luxury of the Great Lord, but I have never seen them erected, not in Constantinople, nor in the field on campaign, when I was among the Turks. I have only seen a few which the sultans presented Emperor Leopold, and which have several poles. They are very heavy, require a lot of work, and it takes a long time to be able to erect them. It is even absolutely necessary to have two similar ones, to always make one stand in front of the other, so that the Sultan finds it erected when he arrives at the camp. This is how all the viziers used it, and the pashas before the rout at Vienna, and those who followed it; but Sultan Mustafa, brother of the one who is on the throne, during the last two campaigns that he made before the Peace of Karlowitz, abolished such great pomp for his tents. Besides, these are not tents whose advantages or inconveniences are unknown, which the Turks have in their camps.

These tents are made of cotton canvas, ordinary canvas, ropes, and are all excellent. They are always lined with another canvas, and most often with a cotton canvas. The round tents, which have only one pole, have at least the upper part of the dome lined. The undercover, which is called in the Imperial Armies the "*marquise*," is also doubled in the small Turkish tents to protect themselves more from the sun, and the rain. The German officers added beams to it, which fall perpendicular to the ground, and which form a kind of gallery between the sides of the tents, which also protected them from heat and cold, and which the Turks then imitated.

The exterior ornaments are almost all green, and the small tassels that hang around are in a checkerboard pattern, and alternately green, and red. Above the poles there is a gilded cast copper ball, and the ropes are mixed in different colors. They are embroidered on the inside with flowers and leaves more or less according to the taste of the owners; and this embroidery is on the lining, which is sometimes of a fine cotton canvas, and sometimes of an orderly striped satin. Sometimes they are also edged with a gold cord: and such was the cabinet[10] in which the Grand Vizier Köprülü spoke to me for three hours before the Battle of Slankamen on the subject of peace. You could not, in truth, see anything more beautiful and more gallant than the ornaments of this cabinet.

The ground is usually covered with a carpet; and the most miserable Turks have at least two sheepskins and cushions of cloth filled with wool. These cushions are sometimes embroidered on all those on which we lean, we put them on wooden platforms that we assemble and disassemble to make them less embarrassing during the marches; and we make little sofas for the convenience of the Turks.

So that we can more easily understand the different figures of the tents of the Turks, I have represented them in Plate XV, where I give a short description. In addition to that in Plates XVI, XVII, and XVIII, I have represented the *Hierogisle*s by which each "*oda*", or Janissary company is distinguished. These figures are on the dome of the tent; and we can see at a glance who they represent when they are erected in a camp. Each of these figures is marked by the number of the company it represents. If some are missing to complete all 190 we cannot assure if they were forgotten in the original Turkish from where I took them, or if these companies are those which are intended for the Sultan's guard and which need not be distinguished by these pompous marks, which are not used after defeats.

---

[10] Translator: The word "cabinet" is that which is used in the original manuscript. At this time a ruler's "cabinet" was where he conducted official business as contrasted to where he slept or ate.

Plate XV

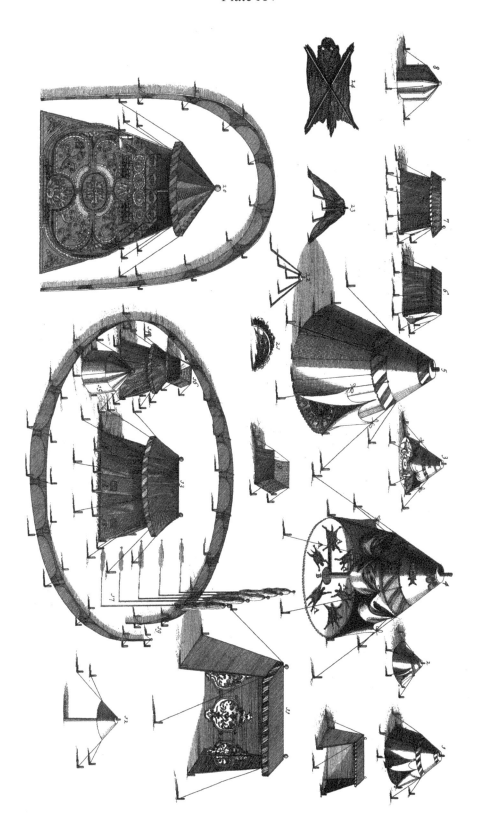

Explanation to Plate XV.

1. Tent of a Janissary company or *od'a*.
2. Cavalry tent, especially the Pracly Cavalry.
3. Janissary *od'a* tent showing sheepskins and eating table around a red Moroccan sofa.
4. The same tent enlarged showing the interior. A. Skins to be sat upon; B. Sofa. One sees outside the figure a red fish in the position where such figures are placed.
5. Janissary tent showing the burse rug.
6. Rectangular "Marquis" tent with no dome.
7. Another Janissary tent in the form known as the "marquis", but which has a peak.
8. The "*corba*" tent without a pole in the middle, whose ticking is waterproof.
9. Wall or screen made with four cloths to cover the latrines.
10. Tent which serves as a shelter and is completely open in the front where the pashas rest and drink coffee.
11. Same as #10, but heavily decorated.
12. Peak supported by a pole, without edging, where the heads of criminals are cut off in public executions.
13. Tent of the "*divan*," where the Grand Vizier holds audiences and eats.
14. Another tent where the Grand Vizier sleeps and where he retires to rest.
15. Another tent where the Grand Vizier sleeps when it becomes cold. It is ticked and embroidered with gold.
16. Screen to cover latrines.
17. Five horse tails that the Grand Vizier raises.
18. Windows to let light into the tent; they are low because the Turks sit on the ground.
19. Entrance of the great cloth screen that is high enough that a man cannot see what occurs inside it.
20. Open tent of the Grand Vizier, with the ground covered with rugs and a sofa. C. placed on raised platforms, covered with a carpet, and having two cushions opposite each side, D, to lean on.
21. Tartar tent covered with shrubs or straw and frequently of horse hide which they kill to eat.
22. Five wooden poles which will lead to a button that the wealthiest Tartars carry on horseback, and where they put their coats, as it is marked in Figure 23.
24. Cowhide spread over two crossed poles which serves the Tartars to put themselves under cover from the sun and rain, by opposing on one side and open on the other.

Symbols of each Oda or Company of Janissaries
That are Shown on the Tops of Their Tents

They are designed with their colors and the number of each company. Several of these symbols have their own significance; others are not so intelligible and represent certain particular things to the Turks; while others, finally, are Turkish characters. I will generally omit the explanation and the translation so as not to bore the reader, even though it is in the Turkish original. They do not display these symbols at the time that they are at the end of the campaign, as I already said.

The Head cook of the Janissaries, 1670's

The Ottoman Army 1683 to 1732

Plate XVI

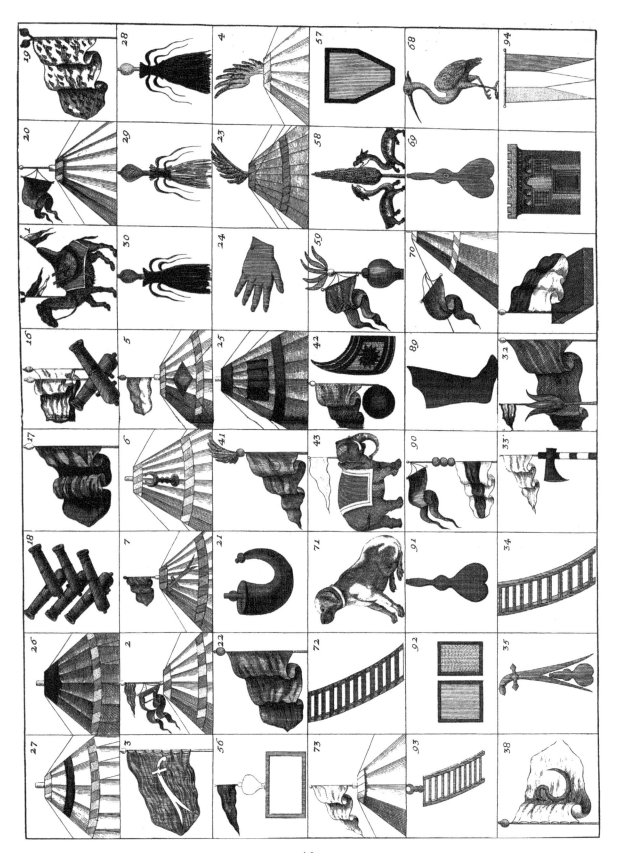

Plate XVII

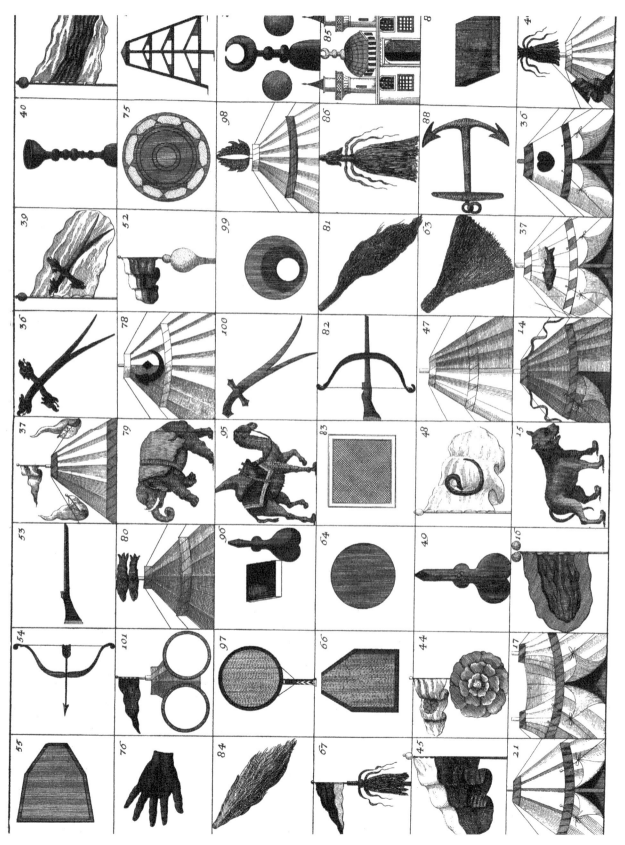

Plate XVIII

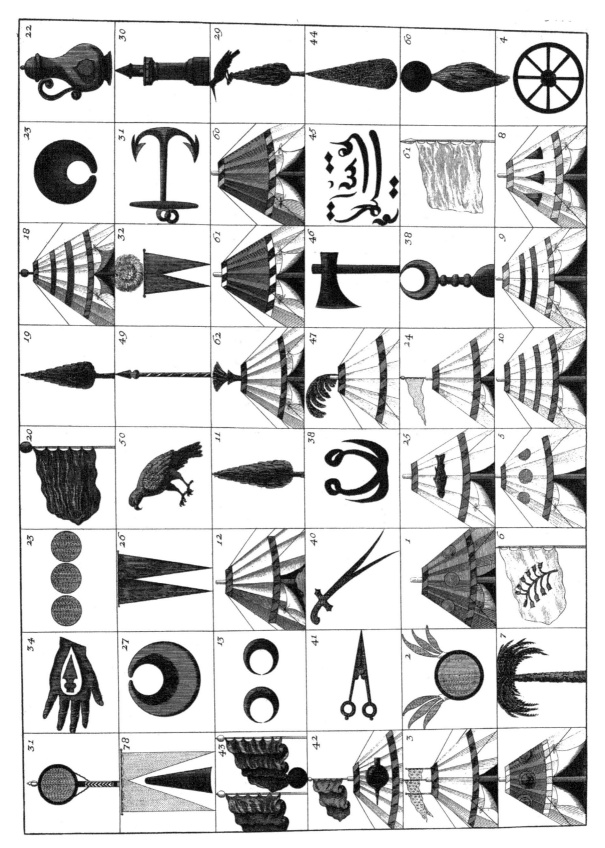

Plate XIX

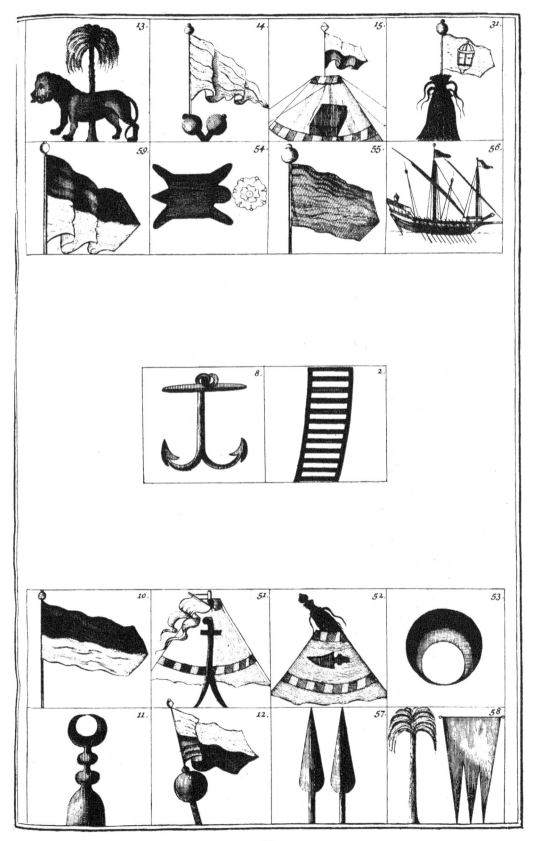

CHAPTER XVII.
Wagons and Pack Animals that Carry the Baggage of the Turkish army

To transport the baggage, of which we have spoken in the previous chapter, the Turks use wagons and pack animals.

To move the heavy baggage, they use four wheeled wagons which are of an equal height and without ironwork, which the treasury rents from peasants for the entire campaign, or those that are provided because of forced contributions. These wagons are drawn by two oxen or two buffalo, as shown in Plate XX.

For the light baggage, they use mules and camels, which I have presented in the same plate.

They also use horses, but as in speaking of those of the cavalry, there are specific sorts, among others which are pack animals.

The mules come for the most part from Anatolia and ordinarily move in groups of seven by seven. This convoy is called a "*katar.*" They all march at the same pace and the same thing is observed with regards to the camels. They are small in comparison to the mules of Italy, but they march incomparably better, when they are loaded proportionally to their size. They follow the steps of the best horse and for the ticklish expeditions they are priceless.

The camels, which the Imperial armies use in great numbers, and which are sold for one *risdale*, although they come from a hot land, full of sand, they find sufficient appropriate food among the Turks. They provide great advantages for the transportation of their baggage, who know how to make saddles appropriate for them.

These animals come in three types and are all called "*deve*," which is Turkish for "camel." The first type of camel is the *maja*, the second is the *luk*, and the third is the *egim*. Those of the first type have a heavy body and handle fatigue well. The second type have more delicate legs, are less fleshy, and have longer muzzles than the first. The third type are like the second but cost infinitely more because they can cost as much as 3,000 or 4,000 *risdales*. They can walk 20 leagues in a day without eating or drinking, and it is for this that they carry the most precious of the baggage. I was told that Kara-Mustafa had some of them at the siege of Vienna (1683) and it was by means of these animals that he saved the *Koran* and the Mohammed Standard.[11] These camels are born in the vicinity of Mecca, and they graze like goats on the leaves and most tender branches of trees. Sometimes they are fed with bread. They can go without drinking, as I have said, because of the province they come from is one of the most arid and sandy, where there are few rivers and fountains, but there are some types of plants that they lick for moisture.

For the most part they come from Thrace, Bulgaria, and Wallachia. They are much smaller than those of Hungary and very slow moving, to which I must add, probably results from the baggage wagons mentioned earlier.

The buffalo come from along the Danube, from all of Bulgaria, Thrace, and Greece and are stronger than oxen, but they are slower. They do not take heat well, and whenever near water they go into it and wallow in mud like pigs. They then rebound, and do not want to be beaten to get out of trouble, and they cannot resist for a long time, when water is lacking to cool themselves, or when they are forced to move. They must keep them so clean and feed them delicately, so that they can only last with those who know

---

[11] Translator: When the Imperial relief force attacked the Turks and freed Vienna, the Poles headed for the Turkish camp. Sobieski thought he had captured the Mohammed Standard, but instead, it was a less significant standard. Kara-Mustafa had seen his army crumbling, packed up the most important parts of his baggage, including the standard, and had fled before the Poles got there.

how to handle them. Hence the peasants take as much care of them as horses. When the Turks had them and camels, they lasted only for a short time because the Turks did not know how to handle them.

One can judge of the movements of an army that has a baggage the size of this of which I have spoken, by the nature of the animals that transport it.

Plate XX.
Explanation to Plate XX.

A. Wagon covered with straw or reed mats.
B. Open wagon, whose wings are made of tree bark.
C. Camel loaded, by which one sees the form of the saddle, the harness, and the banners that it carries, when the Ottoman Army is in its full dress.
D. Loaded mule.

CHAPTER XVIII.
Baggage

We can see from the amount of baggage that the Turks have that they are no longer the Tartars they came from, and that the Tartars that are still part of their army still follow. The baggage of these Tartars, as I said, for each seven or eight people, consists of nothing but a copper boiler, a cloak, which they cover themselves to protect themselves from the insults of the weather, which they join together when they have arrived at the camp, and using tree branches or four poles, which they carry, they make tents for seven or eight. Their vehicle is a pack horse, loaded first of all with a little bit of oats, millet and cooked or salted horse flesh, enclosed in a piece of skin, which, with the reserve of oats, does not weigh 12 pounds. If we consider the horse that carries this baggage, and that of horse they ride, when the first is tired, the load is switched, and he rides the other.

There is no doubt that Erdegrul Morzar of the Turcoman Tartars, did not enter Anatolia with this baggage, with his first army; and that he would be surprised, if he saw the quantity of baggage that the Turks, his descendants, had in their armies, either to feed the soldier with delicacies, or to satisfy them with excessive luxury, which they did during the marches and in their camps during the reign of Muhammad IV.

To give posterity an authentic testimony of what I say, it would suffice to make public the table made by the Procurator Jean Morossni, which is kept in Venice in his palace, which represents the public departure from Constantinople by the Sultan Muhammad IV, under his tents, when he went to besiege Kamieniec. This sultan wished that workers of all the necessary professions and for ordinary use and to the splendor of the army, swell his court. It had never been practiced by any of his predecessors, and we may never see it practiced again by any of his successors. If this picture reaches our nephews, the Ottoman Empire having lost much of its initial splendor, it will allow them to judge how much this Empire is fallen.

We can divide the baggage into six parts, transported, as I said, by carriages or by pack animals.

The first is that which immediately depends on the "*Teftardar-Passa*," who directs the actions of a number of junior officers. This part includes the treasury, divided into purses enclosed in crates covered with goat skin, which they put one on top of the other, in front of the tent called the "*Lalec*," which is the same tent where criminals are beheaded.

To these boxes full of money, we add others full of "*caftan*," a coarse damask that they distribute, according to the usage of the Porte, or to those they want to reward, or to those they want to honor. There are also a lot of Turkish clothes, from shirts to slippers. Grand Vizier Kiuperly[12] presented me with one for my post trip from where he was in Constantinople.

The Imperials often found these treasury boxes, and rarely those of the damask in the victories they won over the Turks.

The second part of the baggage, which is no less in quantity, contains the food, namely the flour to make biscuits, hulled wheat, rice, butter for both grains, oats, mutton and veal; but in less quantity than sheep, for the daily food of the Janissaries and the Kapikulu Cavalry[13], which the Porte must feed, like all the Court, and the Aga of the Grand Vizier, and of the Serasker who commands in place of the Vizier.

The third includes the baggage of the pashas, which is quite considerable. They had doubled it when they came to besiege Vienna, one for the needs of the march, and the other no less rich for the tents, which one day was sent in front with a large number of slaves, so that these heavy flags were erected when they arrived. This was then abandoned after the defeat of Vienna and that of Arsan; they then diminished

---
[12] Köprülüzade Numan Pasha (1670 – 1719)
[13] Kapikulu Sipahi were also known as the Six Divisions of Cavalry were the household cavalry

their luxury and their baggage; however, it is still very considerable today.

It also contains the food of the pashas and that which the *zaims* and *timariots* must carry to feed the soldiers whom they are obliged to lead to the army, in proportion to their income.

The fourth includes food, and the goods that the vivandiers carry to supplement, what is lacking from the provisions of the pashas, *zaims* and *timariots*.

These vivandiers include the workers, who are brought along, either for the needs of the army, or for the pomp. At the siege of Vienna I saw such a prodigious quantity of men, horses, and draft animals, that they appeared to be a formidable army; and yet it was nothing less than that. The last two are for war supplies; under the orders of the *Gebegis-bassy*, or Chief of Munitions, and for the Artillery Corps. Large quantities of munitions and other military stores are carried on nasty peasant carts, as I said. We see in Plate XXIV, several things that relate to this chapter.

CHAPTER XIX.
Food

As I have said, food is considered to be part of the baggage and I shall speak now of the manner in which it is distributed.

The Treasurer pays for the flour, bread, biscuit, rice, the *bulgur* or hulled grain, butter, mutton and beef, and grain for the horses, which is almost all barley.

The bread is not allowed to rise completely, it is all damp, and ready to mold, so the bakers, who are Armenians, make it fresh every day in underground ovens. When the Turks do not have time, or when they are prevented from doing so, they eat the biscuit which is good, and whose stores are full. When they can make bread, they distribute it to each soldier at the rate of 100 *dragmes* per day according to the Imperial Law; they give 50 of biscuit, 60 of beef or mutton, 25 of butter to cook the hulled grain, and 50 of rice every Thursday They give them as much *bulgur*; but only that day at noon, with butter, so they can eat oatmeal.

The Turks distribute these provisions in two places. The meat is issued at the general butchery of the Treasurer, whose butchers are either Greek, or Armenian, or Jewish. Each company sends its kitchen chief, who has a cart and will find the *Meidan-Chiaous* who is, with the list of what is due to each *oda*, in a prominent place. He receives, with his order, the portion of meat due his group weighed out in so many *ockes*.

The distribution of the other food stuffs is done within the *Tefterdar-Bassy*'s enclosure with which is the *Vekil-Karez,* who as the Director of Food, according to the statutes, prepares each consignment. So, everything being brought to the company, the *Vekil-Kare*, divides it up and observes the portions that are missing to be returned to the benefit of the company chest. He gives the rest to the chef, who divides it up for two meals, namely, one for 11 a.m., and the other for 7 p.m. These two meals consist of boiled or steamed meat, where there is sauce with rice, and a little pepper. Oatmeal is never missing on Friday, as I said.

There are six *ouateri*, or kitchen hands, who are used for and are paid at the expense of the *oda*. They appear on solemn days wearing long leather robes, and a large knife hanging from the side inlaid with silver. They serve the food in two copper basins, on a skin rug, called a "*sofa,*" and around which seven or eight people can be seated. I saw this among the tents of the Janissaries.

LAND MILITARY OPERATIONS OF THE TURKS

An Aga of the Janissaries, 1660's

CHAPTER XX
Military Operations of the Turks in General

The clarifications which form the subject of the preceding chapters were, as I have said, necessary to give an idea of the military operations of the Turks, which I have to deal with in this second part. It is time now to enter into the details of these operations and I have said enough to make it easy to understand what they consist of.

By military operations is meant deployment, march, battle, attack, and defense of a fortress. It is necessary to explain how the Turks implement these different kinds of operations; and this will be the subject of the next five chapters, perhaps too abbreviated; because the matter is vast, and each operation in particular would require several chapters.

In spite of this brevity, one will find in the chapter of each operation all the divisions, and subdivisions necessary for a complete clarification, whatever it is under the title of the operation in general. It is true that these chapters will be much longer than the others, but the material is abundant. However, I do not say everything that can be said about it, and I am content to report what seemed to me the most necessary and the most suitable.

CHAPTER XXI.
Encampment

The march of an army seems naturally to be the first military operation; however, I only consider it here as such, when the Turkish army has already formed its camp, and it leaves to go and start hostilities, or to put itself in a state of defense. So, I give precedence to the camp; the Ottoman Army only marches before that time in platoons and without orders; and orders are given only after it has all gone into the camp, which is usually marked in a convenient place, and as far as possible outside the reach of the enemy.

One of the most important and difficult operations of military art is castrametation.[14] It is a matter of choosing the place where the army must encamp; and this place must be convenient and covered from all insults by the enemy. The conveniences of a camp consist in the abundance of water, fodder, and wood, and in their proximity. It is true that one can supply water by digging wells; but for the last two, they absolutely must be at least around the camp. As for safety, either the camp is naturally covered by the layout of the place, or else it is fortified. A naturally fortified camp is one that is found covered on the flanks and rear by a river, a forest, a marsh, or steep mountains. On the contrary, it is fortified either by an entrenchment or by an abatis. In addition, certain general and sometimes certain laws conforming to the views of the general, who proportionate them to the conjunctures that arise, must be observed in castrametation.

The general laws are to have enough ground to place the infantry, the cavalry, the artillery, the provisions, and the officers of each corps with all their baggage; and that the army can conveniently leave the camp to go into battle formation within sight of the enemy. I will speak in this disposition of what I saw the Turks doing either in the time that I was in the Imperial armies, or when I was in some of their camps. I will even give the plan of two or three, and among others of those they formed before investing Vienna, and before the battle of Arsan at Darde on the banks of the Oseck Marsh with regard to Vienna, where the Grand Vizier Suleyman Pasha[15] commanded in person.

There is a master general in the Ottoman Army. Before the Turks lost Hungary, according to the old regulations, when the war was in Europe, this post was held by the *Sangiak*, or *Beg* of Sexar in Hungary. Suleyman, nicknamed "The Great" by the Turks, thus arranged it in favor of the quartermaster who laid out the camp near the Mohacs Plain, where the battle between Louis, King of Hungary, and him took place; and wanted the duties of *Conacgy-Bassy,* or Chief of the Quartiers-Masters, to be held in the person of all those who would succeed the *Sangiakat*.

The battle of Arsan, which the Imperials won over the Turks, at the entrance to the plain of which I have just spoken, avenged the Christians very well for that which King Louis had lost, which was fatal to Hungary. This victory preserved the blockade of Canissa, Siget; Albe-Royale, and d'Agria. One by one these fortresses were starved into submission; and Transylvania, which had passed under Ottoman domination by Suleyman's victory at Mohacs, was returned to its legitimate sovereign the King of Hungary.

This general headquarters having received orders from the Grand Vizier[16] or, failing that, from the

---
[14] Translator: Castrametation – pitching a camp.

[15] Nişanci Suleyman Pasha (? – 1715)

[16] The orders that the Grand Vizier gives on this occasion are voluntary, the Sultan is not informed; and when he leaves Constantinople to go to the army, he very often does not know what to do. The conjunctures, or the situation of the land that will be the theater of the war determine it, when there is a general meeting. On the contrary among Christians, the General of the Army always carries to the camp the plan of operations for the campaign, which previously was settled at the Sovereign's court; and if there is any change in the arrangements, which have been made, they do not touch on the essential elements. The Grand Vizier does everything at will; but still, supposed that the Sultan has resolved to besiege a fortress, if the Vizier does not find it appropriate when arriving at the army, he changes this disposition, and will use his troops in such an expedition that he

Serasker,[17] who is the ordinary General of the Army, and who is with it, although the Grand Vizier is there, will lay out the camp. He is accompanied by all the other quartermasters of the Army, which, if they belong to pashas, are preceded by a hose tail, which is planted in the place where each corps must encamp. There is always an escort for this expedition, although the vanguard is commanded by the *Sarcagy-Bassy* is far enough away to favor, if necessary, a guaranteed retreat to the army.

When we have arrived at the place intended for the camp, the Quartermaster General reads, or has read, the orders he has received for the arrangement of the camp, namely to place the Janissaries and the Serakuli Infantry[18] that we separate from pashas who led it during the approach to the enemy; artillery and all that is necessary to serve it; and finally the posts of the Kapikulu Cavalry and the militia are subject to change. As for the Toprakli Cavalry[19], the military stores, and food wagons, and the Grand Vizier headquarters, their places are almost always uniformly marked in all kinds of camps.

We will examine what is the most advantageous position for all these different corps of the army; and a general maxim for the camp is to leave the following places in the interior. In the first place, the one that must be at the site of the great butchery [slaughterhouse], both for the infantry, cavalry, gunners, and gunsmiths, as for the court of the Grand Vizier; and distribute the grain, the butter for the oatmeal, and the oats for the horses. The second place is that of the Janissaries, the Serakuli Infantry, the artillery and the gunners. These compartments, subject to change, are visible, as are those that must be fixed. There is no quarter master daring enough to dare to take possession of the area assigned to these troops, before the tent where criminals are killed is erected, and there is displayed behind one of the horse tails of the Grand Vizier. This must be the model; also, as soon as this horse tail is posted, the master quarters are adjusted there to display those of the pashas according to the rank which belongs to them, either on the right or on the left on two wings, observing, however, that they make a type of circle that contains all the other parts of the camp.

They try as much as possible to place the infantry close to the water intended for the service of the army, and this is for two reasons. The first is that the Turks do not drink wine, and they necessarily need water to quench their thirst; and the second is that they also need it to purify themselves the night before prayer. Added to this they also have the habit of washing after having made their necessities[20] behind certain canvas walls, which I spoke of in the chapter on tents. This lavishness of water is counterbalanced, by the care of wood, which they consume very little of; they dig small stoves in the ground, which costs them only a moment of work, and with the smallest twigs, dry grass, and even dried cattle droppings, they heat water for cooking.

---

may judge as appropriate, without giving notice to the Sultan. It is true that if he is unlucky in his affairs, he risks paying with his head for the failure of the expedition; but the Turks care very little about that. In a battle, he always commands the Reserve Corps, and rarely is he seen giving his orders in the fray.

[17] The *Serasguier* is Commander-in-Chief in the absence of the Vizier; but his power is subordinated to that of this prime minister; he must take orders on leaving for the army, and not deviate from them. If the difficulties, which arise in operations, require a change in the layout of the campaign plan, he is obliged to give notice by letters to the Grand Vizier, who sends him new orders to act on the occasion. He assembles the Divan in the camp (this is the Turkish Council of War, and he decides on the points that are not of great importance). If he is alone in the army, he commands at the post of honor in a battle; but if the Grand Vizier is there, he only commands one of the wings, at his choice, and responds with his head to the Vizier for any failure. Often a vizier who fails in an action blames it on the *Serasker*, who is then the unfortunate victim who is sacrificed for the honor of this prime minister.

[18] Levy troops of the Empire

[19] Equivalent of feudal cavalry

[20] Translator: In Muslim cultures at this time, when they defecated, they used their left hand to clean themselves. They used their right hand to reach into the common food bowls and the left hand was *never* to be used to eat, for obvious reasons.

For the arrangement of the tents, they have no procedure; they are confused and without order, so that the exit is sometimes on the right, sometimes on the left; and although those of the pashas are distinguished by a horse tail that marks it, they are not, however, erected in any better order, which I myself noticed.

Having been made a slave by the Ottoman Army when it besieged Vienna, I lived near the village of Brandkirken in this vast plain where the penultimate camp was, before the fortress was invested in a circular camp. The infantry and cannon were in the front, as shown in Plate XXVI, little different from XXIV, which shows the camp of the Grand Vizier Suleyman Pasha who commanded the most beautiful and largest army that the Turks had since that which besieged Vienna, and which was then defeated at the battle of Arsan. I had these plans drawn up in Constantinople by a Turk who had the plan, with the names of some pashas; and I found that the shape of these two camps was quite similar to that which the Vizier Kiuperly had erected near Belgrade, where the vanguard was camped beyond the Sava which it had passed over a bridge, and especially for the headquarters.

It is on the plan of these plates that the demonstrations that I am going to make are directed, so that everyone can judge to their fancy.

I have seen more than one Turkish camp, at the time when the Imperials won over them such great and important victories. However, I could never understand anything about it in terms of form, since the joy that victory gives brought confusion, and these camps were destroyed by the looting that followed. For the two which I have just mentioned above, it is not the same; I had the time to examine them, besides that I had the plan in Constantinople; and I hold, from more than one Turk to whom I have spoken of it, what I have reported.

I have seen, I say, several Turkish camps; but they were covered by the army arranged according to their order of battle, or by confusedly laid out entrenchments; and with the exception of the Grand Vizier's tents, which could be distinguished, nothing could be assured of the Janissaries.

Their camp in front of Vienna, where I was a slave from the opening of the trench, until the Turkish defeat, with the infantry reserve, which was encamped close to the trench, and of the headquarters of the Grand Vizier which was a little behind, narrow only a confused and incredible heap of all kinds of paraphernalia. This came from the pride of the Grand Vizier who wanted to impose it on the Christians whose strength he despised.

I will divide what I have just said, by counting all the parties that make up the camps mentioned above; and I begin with that of Suleyman Pasha on the banks of the Ozeck Marsh, to which I add what has been said to me, in addition to what is marked on the drawing of Plate XXI.

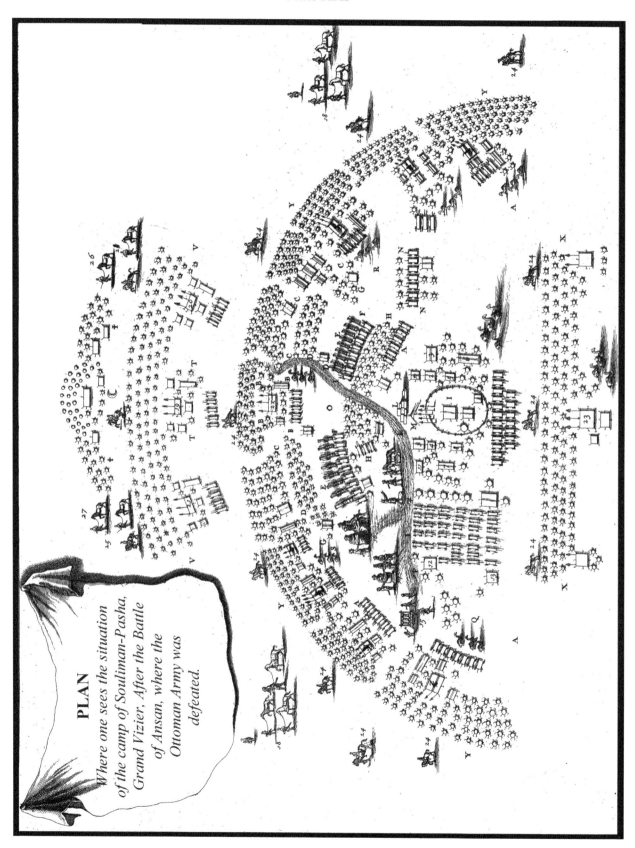

Explanation to Plate XXI.

AAAA.	Headquarters general, or the tent of the Grand Vizier or of the army commander is in the middle, surrounded by the tents listed below
B.	Quarters of the *Serasker*.
CCCCCC.	Quarters of the paid Kapikulu Cavalry, divided into the left and right wings. The two wings formed of the Seratkuli Infantry.
DDDDDD.	Artillery arranged in two wings.
EE.	Line of ammunition wagons.
F.	Two little quarters of the cannoneers.
GGGG.	Quarters of the Janissaries with the horses and mules that handle their baggage.
H.	Great street to go to the Provisions Quarter, which serves as a market.
I.	Stacked Treasury chests.
L.	Tents for executions.
M.	Quarter for the heavy military stores.
NN.	Place to serve the artillery.
O.	Slaughter yard and food distribution point.
P.	Enclosure for animals carrying food and cattle, and butchers' baggage.
Q.	Others in the vicinity of the reserve powder magazine, where the Janissaries began to organize to march.
R.S.	Tartar quarters.
TT.	Quarter called the "*cialegy*," or the vanguard commanded by pashas, being Saly, Pasha of Damascus, who is the chief of the two others, by Delayer, Pasha of Anatolia, and by Osman, Pasha of Romelia.
VV.	Quarter of the rearguard, called the "*dondan*," commanded by Jeghen Pasha, with 4,000 horse.
XX.	Line of circumvallation formed by the Toprakli Cavalry or the provincial cavalry, which are the *timariots, zaims,* and pashas of the Empire, who encamp behind their soldiers, as indicated by the letter Z, and who leave between space to form a separation as shown in the diagram.
YYY.	

The line of circumvallation though round is divided into the right and left wing, which join to the quarters of the *Serasker*, marked B, and the two other wings of the Kapikulu Cavalry, marked C.C.

Explanation of the Subdivisions

1. Tents of the Grand Vizier, the first where he holds audiences, the second which is behind, where he rests on hot days, and the round, third one, is where he sleeps.
2. Tent of the *Chiaja* of the Grand Vizier.
3. Tent of the *Reis-Efendi*, or Chancellor.
4. Tent of the *Chiaous-Bassy,* around which are those of the other *chiqus*.
5. Tent of the Squire of the Grand Vizier.

6. Long tent that serves as a stable for the horses of the Grand Vizier.
7. Another tent that is the Grand Vizier's kitchen.
8. Tent of the executioner.
9. Tent of the *tefterdar-pasha*, surrounded by those of the court officers.
10. Tent where the standard and the vest of Mohammed are guarded. There are always lit lamps and the Turks who wear a green turban, like that of the Prophet's race, as well as the pashas of the Grand Vizier, who prays there. Some Kapikulu cavaliers are there to guard it as well as the treasury.
11. Tent of the *chiaja* of the *Tefterdar-Pasha*, who is there to observe the orders regarding provisions.
12. Tent of the *zagargy-bassy* or Commissioner of Provisions.
13. Tent of the *chiaja*, who takes care of the distribution of food.
14. Tent of the *meidan-chiaqus*. It is on a hillock, in order that this officer, who has the roll of all the corps that the Sultan's treasurer must furnish food, to verify it, in case of doubt that the commissioners deceived him.
15. Butchery where the commissioners go to pick up meat.
16. Sacks, with which they distribute grain and oats.
17. Place where they pick up butter.
18. Advanced guards of the camp, dismounted cavaliers holding their horses by the bridal, but the vedettes are on horse.
19. Tent of the *Cialcagy*, or Pasha of the vanguard. This was Saly, Pasha of Damascus.
20. Tent of Osman, Pasha of Romelia.
21. Tent of Delaver, Pasha of Anatolia.
22. Tent of Chiaqus Pasha, *Serasker*, or Commander-in-Chief of the Army.
23. *D'Jeghen Pasha Dondar Oserchiume*, or Grand Commander of the Rearguard formed of 4,000 men.
24. All the horse drummers, who make the rounds during the night, drumming their great drums and crying out in honor of Mohammed, and desires for the prosperity of the Sultan.
††† Quarter of the Moldavians on the right, the Wallachians on the left, and the Kam of the Tartars with his soldiers.
25. Tartar Guards where the soldiers dismount to hold their horses by the bridal and the horse vedettes.
26. Advanced guard of the Moldavians, dismounted, and holding their horses by the bridal.
27. Wallachians.

I shall begin in the center where one finds the tent of the Grand Vizier; or that of whomever commands in his place. One of the five horse tails, who the Vizier raises in front of his tent serves, as I have already said, the guide by which all the corps of troops who form the Ottoman Army should arrange themselves when encamping.

There is a sufficient description of the various types of tents in the previous chapters, as well as the number of wagons, pack and draft animals, and artillery, which form such a vast camp such as that of an Ottoman army.

One can see here the amount of ground occupied by a general headquarters in a camp marked A.A.A.A.; the tent of the Grand Vizier or army commander is in the middle and those of the necessary officers are around it. It is an order that is generally obeyed in any Turkish camp. All these tents are all covered in the explanation of their design so that one can easily, find, without distraction, the principal parts of a camp.

From this center we form a sort of other larger one, around which the quarters of the pashas from the provinces which have their cavalry form a circumference. It should be noted, however, that in camps of this nature, when one is in the sight of enemy, the Serakuli Infantry of all the pashas take their own quarters, close to that of the Janissaries, the artillery and the ammunition. There are between the district of each pasha certain interrupted spaces, which the different kinds of militia leave, to mark the separation which is a rule established among the Turks for organizing their encampments.

This second center forms the front and the sides of the camp. The Serasker has his post in the front; in the camp of which I speak, this officer was named Chiaous Pasha; and its quarter is marked B. There was on the right and on the left of this quarter, between the line of the Toprakli Cavalry, all the paid Kapikulu Cavalry, whose quarter is distinguished by the right-wing, and the left-wing, as C.C. All the Serakuli Infantry formed two others from behind marked D.D. These two wings, as we can see on the plan, covered the artillery also ranged on wings marked E.E., with a line formed by the ammunition carts marked F., the others in greater numbers having been reserved for another position than I will indicate in its time

The G. G. gunners' quarters are at the end of the two artillery wings; and that of the Janissaries, marked H. with all their baggage carts and the mules which carry their tents, is behind. This last district of the Janissaries is divided in two by the large street I. which leads to the place where the food is distributed, under the direction of the Tepterdar-Pasha; which serves at the same time as a market place, where one sells food, and the goods of which I spoke of in the chapter on baggage. This street is opposite the treasury marked L. and the execution tent marked M., so that everyone has in front of him, in passing, the rewards and the punishments that they might receive.

The main part of the military stores is put aside in the place marked N. N.; and we spot that there is always a place all around, in case that the fire takes there, that Turks can more easily guarantee the camp.

We see in this vicinity the following places, marked O. P. Q. R. S.

The first O. is to serve artillery.

The second P. serves as a butcher's shop; and food is distributed there.

The third Q. is used to contain the draft animals, and those needed for the butchery. Sheep are kept there especially, and even away, to protect them from looting, which is why there is always a guard; and finally, so that they have good pastures.

The fourth and fifth R.S., which are around the magazine with reserve gunpowder, are used by the Janissaries, for them to gather, and it is there that they begin to line up, albeit confusedly, to prepare for the march.

A similar arrangement in a camp present as much to the eye in the field, as the design on paper. Such an extent first makes it appear that the army is much more numerous than it actually is; to which must be added all the pompous display of tents as I reported above. However, we see from what I have pointed out about empty spaces, and yet necessary for the particular uses of the Turks, and their prodigious amount of baggage, that it is necessary to reduce the prejudices that give the first life of their camps. These large empty spaces are so necessary that without them the militia, as well as the baggage, would be in a kind of labyrinth and prison, as one can judge by Plate XXII, attached.

Plate XXII.

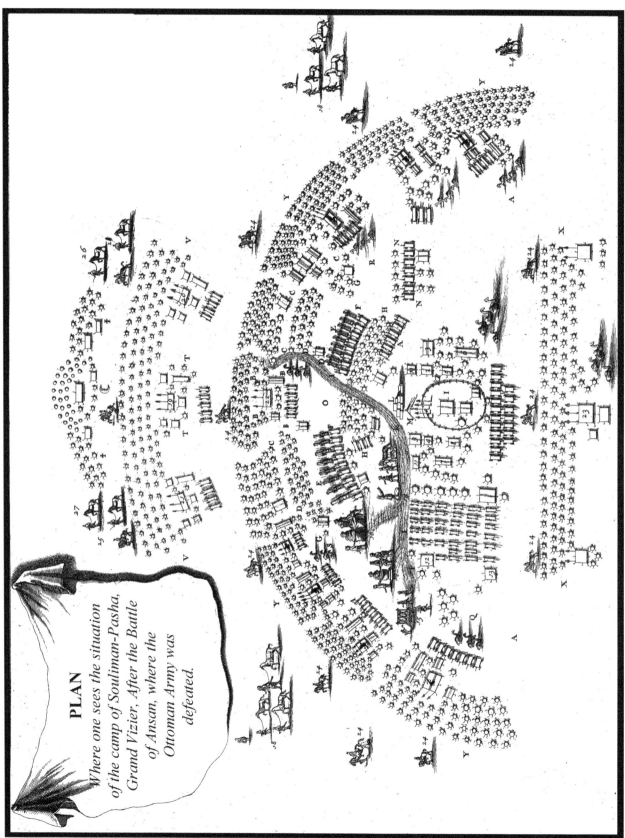

Explanation of Plate XXII.

Here one sees a portion of a Turkish cavalry camp, by which one can judge that it is a true labyrinth, be it to enter or to exit; and as much for the Turks as for the Christians who might wish to attack it.

A. Tent of the horsemen.
B. Barrier of planks which serves as a trough for the horses, in order that they cannot spoil the fodder.
C. Depression dug for a type of oven to boil oatmeal.
D. Tents that serve as walls around the latrines, which consist of large depressions; there is one opening such that one can judge their size.

One can judge by this sample, where we see only hollow stakes and planks in confusion, if all this paraphernalia is not very inconvenient in a camp for the Turks themselves. There are also sometimes wagons mixed in, which increases the confusion, and which I have only omitted not to further confuse this illustration. To this must be added all the tent ropes, and those whose horses are tied by the leg to the stakes.

The infantry camp is subject to many of the same inconveniences, with the exception of the barriers for the horses, which are there in a very small number, but there are some for the officer's horses and the draft and pack animals, E.

I have put in this diagram some of the small tents of the horsemen, so that we can see how the horses are attached to the stakes. These tents serve at least for three or four riders; and if the weather and the situation of the place allow it, they make a barrier in front, so that the horses do not tread on the forage. They tie the horse by one of the hind legs to the stake, and thus make a kind of labyrinth, whose awkwardness increases by the small ovens intended for cooking, and the large hollows of latrines whose number is excessive, which they cover with canvas, or thick branches and foliage. All these impediments makes the camp almost inaccessible, especially at night, to the Turks themselves, and infinitely more to the enemy who would like to surprise them.

I have experienced what I say. The Imperials having won the battle of Vidin, the victorious soldiers could not restrain their impetuosity to enter the Turkish camp. The right wing of the Turkish army, which had already fled, noticed that a large number of German horsemen started to enter the camp on foot to loot it. Suddenly these Turks came upon them; and it is certain that without the prompt help brought by Prince Louis of Baden, who then commanded the Imperials, and General Veterani, the Turks would have cut them to pieces. They were so stopped by the embarrassment of the ropes and the hollows that they could neither rally nor get out of such a labyrinth; and there were even several who abandoned their horses and fled on foot to the Imperial camp.

Until the campaign of 1687, the Turks always supported their camp by another flying camp, which was six leagues from the main camp, which was composed of the elite of the Toprakli Cavalry. This camp was preceded by another six leagues by the whole body of the Tartars, who formed another; and the tributary militias of Moldova and Wallachia were on the wings and formed their flanks.

The rearguard was made up of another flying camp but was much weaker than the vanguard marched four or five leagues, and sometimes six, leagues to the rear of the main body of the army. Some small corps were detached from it to escort the carts of the sick, and those whose cattle were tired.

The Grand Vizier Kara Mustafa, who besieged Vienna, used this vanguard, which is called a *"cialcagy"* in Turkish. Because it was this body of the Ottoman Army, which under the orders of Mehmet

Pasha, and the Kam of the Tartars made this great foray into the Lower Austria. This troop encamped in the order that the plate shows, according to which first quarter of the Tartars is marked T.T. It is very far from the main body of the army, with the other two designated by H., namely to the right of the Moldavians and to the left of the Wallachians. It is rare that the Tartars having their quarter with that of the Turks in the Ottoman Army, S. if that happens, it must be in a very urgent case.

The district marked V. V. is that of the vanguard called "*cialcagy*." Three pashas commanded it, namely Saly, Pasha of Damascus, Delaver, Pasha of Anatolia, and Osman, Pasha of Romelia. The rearguard is called a "*dondar*." It contains 4,000 men and was commanded by Jeghen Pasha, the same who rose to the rank of pasha by the reputation he gained as a brave warrior while working as an assassin on the great roads of Anatolia. Sultan Mahomet granted him mercy on the condition that he fight in Hungary, which he did. This favor was recognized; the Sultan having been deposed, he formed a party in his favor, of which he made himself chief against the rebels of Constantinople, who had deposed him; and even against the will of the new monarch, he declared himself Serasker. I could report here many very curious things on this subject; but that would move away for my intentions for this work.

The Camp of the Grand Vizier Kara Mustapha Pasha in the Brandkirken Plain, before the siege of Vienna, was in the same form as the previous one, as we can see by Plate XXIII.

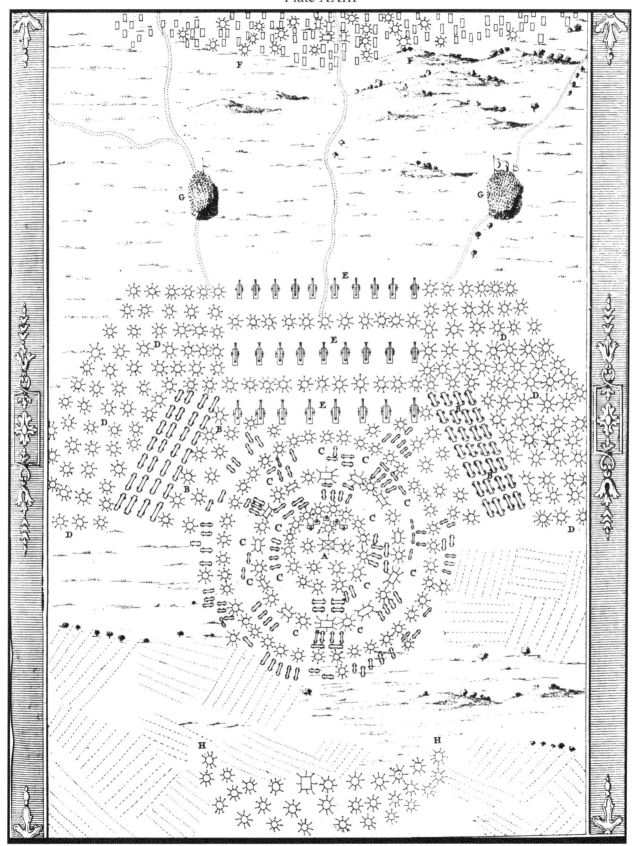

Explanation of Plate XXIII.

Here we see the camp of the Grand Vizier Kara Mustapha Pasha one day from Vienna in the Brandkiraten plain before he went to besiege the city.

Neither the streets nor the squares are marked in this camp, which is the custom of the Turks to make there; and I did not know if those who laid it out wished it thus or if they forgot to do so. However, it might well have been done in this way, so that the Army was more compact that night.

A.	Camp Center formed by the Tent of the Grand Vizier
1.	Tent where executions are made.
2.	Treasurer's cases.
B.B.	Two wings formed by the Kapikulu Cavalry.
C.C.C.C.	Carts for military supplies and food.
D.D.D.D.	Toprakli Cavalry or provincial pashas.
E.E.E.	Line formed by artillery, Janissaries and Toprakli Infantry
F.F.	Vanguard
G.G.	Two Cavalry corps, whose horses are saddled, and placed between the headquarters and the vanguard quarter.
H	Quarter of the rearguard.

The posts of the vanguard and rearguard are always positioned as I have indicated until 1687, when Suleyman Pasha commanded the Ottoman Army and who organized his camp according to that plan that I have given. It was he who had begun first to draw back the two-army corps into the camp, leaving the Tartars outside it to make raids, and that they entrenched themselves first when they encamped near Oseck. The plan of this entrenched camp is presented in Plate XXIV.

Plate XXIV

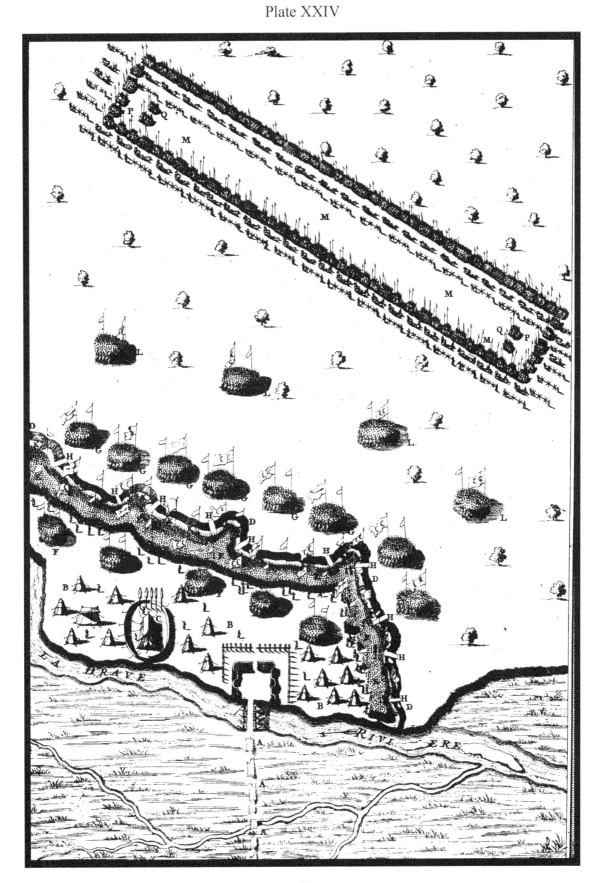

Explanation of Plate XXIV.

This plate shows the march of the Imperial army, under the orders of His Serene Highness, Prince Charles, Duke of Lorraine,[21] in front of Oseck, on the side of Slavonia to urge the Ottoman Army to accept battle. It was not known then that it was entrenched around Oseck, under the orders of Suleyman Pasha.

The Imperials passed the Drava a little above Valcovar, five leagues from Osek, and left their baggage there.

Oseck was then hardly more than a stockade; the army had to pass there to reach this beautiful wooden bridge of an extreme length which led either to the village opposite of Darda, crossing a marsh formed by the waters of the Drava, which when the snow melts in the Alpes floods and causes the Danube to flood and emerging from its bed overflows those banks barely two leagues from Germany. The Imperials burned this bridge when Buda was taken; and the Turks, to prevent the flooding, made an earthen dam there; the remains of the bridge are marked A. A. A.

- B.   Turkish camp.
- C.   Grand Vizier's tent.
- D.D.D.D.   This Turkish entrenchment was the first they had made, which the Imperials saw with a telescope as it is marked, which they then knew about after the capture of Oseck
- E.   Infantry that was around this entrenchment
- F. F. F. F.   Main body of cavalry which was behind the infantry.
- G.G.G.G.   Corps of cavalry which were pell-mell around the entrenchment, from which they had come out, through the openings and the tongues of earth, left in the ditch, and marked H. H. H. H., which had at the beginning a small cross marked I.I.I.I.

- K.K.K.K   The cannon was placed as seen on badly constructed trunnions.
- L.L.L.L.   Four other corps of cavalry that were watching the march of Imperials as they approached, who even refrained from attacking them, which would have broken the order of battle of the army. They did not, however, leave their post, and preferred to suffer the fire from the Turkish cannon, which were being entrenched, even though they were very inconvenienced.

The fields between the two armies, and even around, were filled with brushwood, which, however, did not prevent the Emperor's army from remaining in order; while the sappers of each regiment were busy cutting the brush.

- M. M.   The Imperial army, composed of infantry and cavalry arranged in the ordinary order, and the cavalry divided by squadrons, and the infantry by battalions; and in alternatives the lines were formed by a battalion and two squadrons; and before each battalion there were two artillery pieces called regimental cannons.

---

[21] Translator: Prince Charles of Lorraine commanded the army that broke the Turkish siege of Vienna in 1683.

The whole army arranged in this order formed two wings, the first marked N.N. and the second O.O. It as enclosed by two flanks P.P. and behind the flanks was a corps of dragoons marked Q.Q., which sometimes left their post to run against the enemy, however far away from the army body.

The front of each line was seconded by the movement of the artillery, which appeared, like the two flanks, and more outside cannon range was the line of chevaux de frise, which pairs of infantry carried on their shoulders, which formed a line as shown in the figure, so that in an instant the Imperials could put them on the ground and link them together.

It was in this order that the army stopped within range of the cannon, opposite that of the Turks, entrenched as I said, and that to everyone's amazement, it did what it could to engage the Grand Vizier to give battle. But he did not budge from his entrenchments, and he withdrew at the slightest sign that part of his cavalry which was outside.

The Imperial army would have moved too far, by attacking the Turks in their entrenchments, from its stores, and from its baggage, which were on the Drava, by firing on the side of the Danube. His Serene Highness of Lorraine liked it better, seeing that the army lacked water, to make this beautiful retreat, which I would have drawn with points on the plate, if its size had allowed me, with the pursuit of the Turkish Cavalry which never dared to come to an attack, seeing such a beautiful, orderly retreat.

Charles, Duke of Lorraine, who had passed the Drava far above Oseck, did not follow his plan to attack Suleyman. He saw that he would have stretched his left wing too far on the Drava, that he was exposing the bridge and the magazines he had brought over this river, and that he would risk running out of water that night, if he moved to within sight of the Turkish camp the next day. This great captain executed a retreat which deserves to be written by some man skillful in the military art and take an honored place in history. The Turks judged by this maneuver that the Imperials were fleeing, seeing no difference between fleeing in a terrified panic, and withdrawing in battle order. In the thought that the Imperial army feared them, they wanted to charge, but it was useless, the retreat was made in the most beautiful order ever seen.

The whole Ottoman Empire resounded with praise for the entrenchments that had prevented the Imperials from attacking them; and it was published there that the Turks had finally found the means of subduing the Germans. These entrenchments were used, not only in all the following campaigns, as I will relate, but also the same Vizier Suleyman Pasha who wanted to cross the Drava by coming to Darda, took refuge again on the banks of the Oseck Marsh as I have said, by forming the camp shown on Plate XXIV, and with his army reinforced by the vanguard, and the rear guard advanced near Arsan. From there he discovered that of the Imperials were among the woods and began the entrenchments that we see in Plate XXV.

Plate XXV.

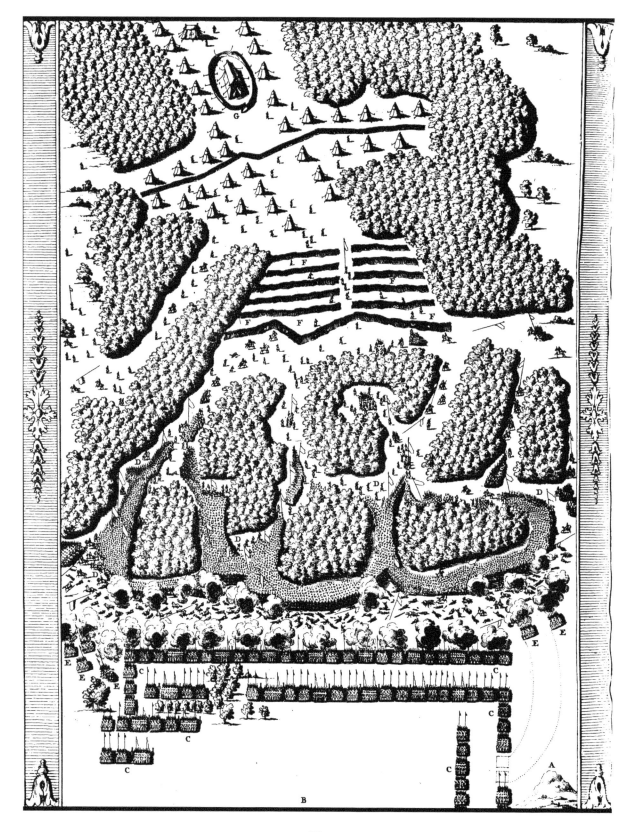

Explanation of Plate XXV.

If one examines the plan of the battle that His Serene Highness Prince Charles fought with the Grand Vizier Suleyman Pasha, at the foot of Mount Arsan, at the beginning of the Mohacs plain, in coming to Oseck. This plain was unfortunate for his situation, when the loss of this battle which took the name, and which, with Hungary, cost the life of the king. It was then the cause of the recovery of this kingdom, Transylvania, and the complete decay of the Ottoman Empire and the deposing of Sultan Mahomet.

- A.   Mount Arsan.
- B.   Beginning of the Mohac Plain.
- C.C.   The Imperial army, arrayed in battle formation in two lines. This army was marching to break the siege of Siclos.
- D.D.D.D.   The Ottoman army consisted almost completely of infantry posted as it appears here, in the defiles of the forest that abuts the Oseck Marsh. It began attacking the Imperials, which it put to flight by their cannon fire and musketry, and which, then pressed by the Turks, was reinforced by the squadrons initially on the flanks marked E.E.E.E., which the movement is designated by the punctuated lines and then by the battalions of infantry, when the Turks fled in disorder on the side of their entrenchments, marked F.F.F.F. in the place which is in the middle of the forest.

Their camp was covered by the entrenchments, of which I have spoken; and there was another which served to cover their retreat and which covered the Grand Vizier's tent marked G. This camp, which was the largest since Vienna, which the Imperials captured it, included the artillery and baggage.

This Vizier imagined that in this meeting the Duke of Lorraine would flee, as he had done at Oseck, where he made such a fine retreat; but he was mistaken. His Serene Highness had his army placed in battle formation and was ready to fight the Turks. The Turkish cavalry fled first, and left the Janissaries, the artillery, the baggage, and, in a word, the whole camp was soon at the mercy of the victor. Since the defeat of the Ottoman army before Vienna, the Imperials had not seen a camp as rich and as pompous as this one; and there was no victory more advantageous to Christianity, and more fatal at the same time to the Turks.

Although they realized at the beginning that this way of covering their camp was not very advantageous for them, since they had been defeated, they did not stop following the same process during the following campaigns. As soon as they felt the Imperials approaching, they took refuge; but that did not prevent them from being routed, as I will report in detail, even giving the design of the main actions.

This first camp was set up according to the ancient custom of the Turks; and the second differed in this very little from the first. I will however finish the examination of the camp of Suleyman Pasha which I have described to pass to that of the Camp of Kara Mustafa, a day's march from Vienna.

I have spoken of the differences in places, which are in these camps, necessary for the Turks for the movements of their army, which are always done with much confusion, whether they put themselves in a state of defense, or whether they attack their enemy.

Those who understand what castrametation [pitching camp] is, will easily understand at the sight of the diagram that I gave of the Turkish camps, that they claim to take advantage of the Toprakli Cavalry. This cavalry is that of the pashas of the Empire, and is more or less numerous, depending on the number of Ziamets and Timars that each pasha has in his department. When it is joined to the Tartars, and to the militia of the tributary states, all this together forms in various distances around the shared camp, as I said, a kind of line of circumvallation of cavalry, reinforced by two others more advanced and at least six leagues apart, and more, if possible.

The most advanced corps is that of the Tartars, Moldavians and Wallachians; the other of several thousand Turks is the Zagargy Quarter, and the third is that of the rearguard, a few thousand horse strong. All these corps stand in their particular camp, until they find themselves forced by the enemy's approaches to withdraw and reinforce the line of circumvallation of which I spoke.

This is how the Turks successfully waged war in Asia. They had none the less in Europe against the Rascians, the Bulgarians and the Hungarians, nations which differed little from them, in the manner of fighting. This way of fighting, and of keeping the cavalry close, either by attacking or by defending with a firm footing, earned them the conquests that we have seen that they have made on different occasions.

The Janissaries, who have so often experienced in Hungary that, whether they were in the front, or whether they were on the flanks of the army, the cavalry never supported them, so that they take cover in entrenchments, and behind baggage wagons; and they remain there, until the cavalry has fled, which makes them judge that the army is routed.

Indeed, if the cavalry, which forms such a prodigious line of circumvallation, held fast, and withstood the shock of the German troops, as it did, while fighting against the nations named above, the army could, as it did before, leave the camp, under the escort of the cavalry; and the infantry, the artillery, and in a word all the baggage would be covered.

The advanced guards, arranged around a camp which is in front of the enemy, ensure its tranquility. The Turks take enough precautions on this side; not only by the post that they make take with their vanguard and rearguard, numbering, as I said, several thousand men; but they still have the camp guards, which consist of vedettes, posted from distance to distance. These vedettes take care to keep the soldiers alert during the night, while making their rounds around the camp. There are also drummers posted between the camp and the vedettes, who beat the large drums that I spoke of in the chapter on musical instruments of war. These drummers are on horseback; and as they are beaten, they shout for joy in honor of God, the Prophet Mohammed and the Sultan.

There are hardly any tents in the camp, or a baggage cart, where during the night some slave who does not cry out from time to time the alert.

We now come to the description of the camp represented in Plate XXVI. It is the one that was erected one day's march from Vienna in the Brandkirken Plain.

It was in this plain, that the Grand Vizier wanted to have his quarters, and the treasury indicated by No. 2, was in front of his tent marked A. which served as the center, in the small circles formed by those of the officers of his court, and the lines described by the cavalry. The flanks were supported by two other lines, one formed by the Janissaries and marked B, and the other by the Serakuli Infantry, which was itself covered by the baggage wagons marked C. The pashas' cavalry, marked D, defended the baggage, and the artillery, marked E, and was arranged in the same manner as it appears on purpose, covered the front of the camp. The vanguard, marked F, was a few leagues away, facing Vienna, and a bit of it appears on this illustration; and the detached cavalry corps marked G. were between the camp and the rearguard.

We see in this camp, quite different from all the others, the places that the Turks want to have there; and, as I have reported, they had tightened them here around the headquarters of the Grand Vizier, to make the camp tighter, and at the same time more in a state of defense. The rearguard is marked H.

We can easily understand the look presented by a camp, where more than half of their numbers were located, showed only luxury and wealth; and where the number of merchants, and slaves, infinitely exceeded the number of soldiers. To which we must add that all the tents were new, and of the latest cleanliness; and that the baggage train was the most magnificent that the Ottoman Empire had ever produced.

I return to the castrametation of the Turks. They soon began to form from time-to-time trunnions, of this earth which was drawn from the ditch dug without any order to make the entrenchment. These trunnions served as a battery to store the barrels; and the two flanks of these trunnions were left with an opening for entering and leaving the entrenchment; and these openings were still covered by a traverse. It will not be difficult to understand all this, as long as we can understand it, by casting our eyes on the diagram.

All these entrenchments served little purpose, for lack of knowing how to direct them. But it does not suit me to go into any detail, and I will confine myself to speaking of the attacks which they suffered on the part of the Imperials, on the occasions where it was found good, to attack them in their entrenchments.

The entrenchment at Oseck which we see in Plate XXVI was not attacked by Duke Charles of Lorraine, for the reasons which I have already reported.

That which the same Suleyman Pasha made, after having withdrawn from under the cannon of Arsan, to come to Darda, was nothing other than a boyau, and dug without order, or measure. We see the form in Plate XXVIII. This retrenchment, which was in the woods, and among the undergrowth was made by the Janissaries in the anticipation that the cavalry would flee. Which did not happen; the Imperials forced the entrenchment, and became masters of the camp, where everything in it was at their disposal, both artillery and baggage.

Arat-Pasha, this Serasker, who had been beaten in the plain which is in front of Patacin, dug an entrenchment within sight of Nissa, such as one sees in Plate XXVI

Plate XXVI.

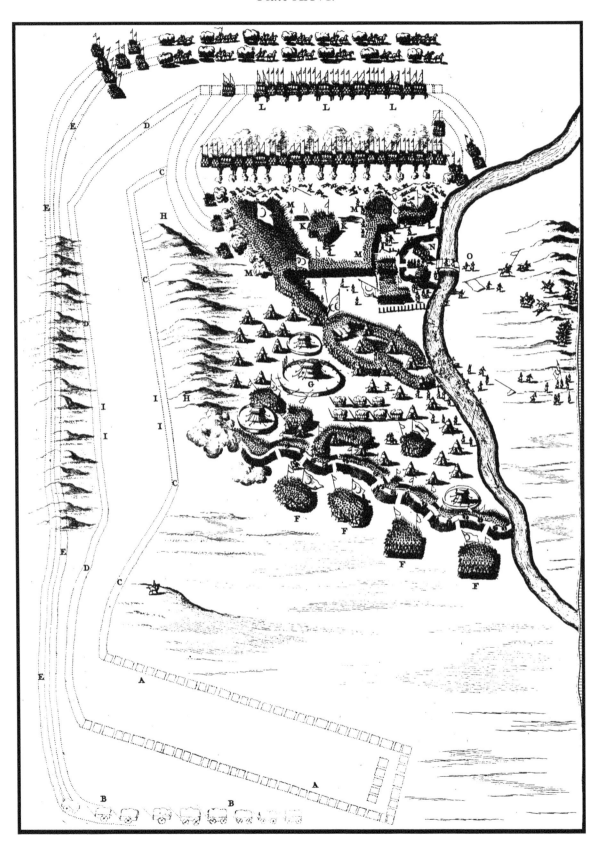

Explanation of Plate XXVI.

This plate shows the order of battle of the Imperial army commanded by His Serene Highness, the Prince Louis of Baden, the day before the Battle of Nissa, the army having stood all the previous night under arms, without setting up camp, and entrenching that Arat Pasha, Serasker of the Porte had done to enclose his army encamped around Nissa, and covered on the flank on the right by a certain hill, and on the left by the Nissa River. We can also see the march that the Imperial army took the next day to take the Turks' in the rear, without their being able to use their entrenchments.

A.A.	Imperial army ranged in battle according to its ordinary custom, and marked with dots, which show how, it passed the night before the battle.
	Baggage situation.
B.B.	Path marked by the first Imperial Line before the battle
C.C.C.C.	March of the second line of the Imperials, made in the valley itself which is between the two chains of hills marked in the diagram.
D.D.D.	
E.E.E.E.	Two lines of the baggage marching, which goes up to the top of the vineyard covered hillsides, the path being made by sappers of the regiments and some pioneers.
	The Ottoman army always remained in the same situation as it was in its entrenchments, that is to say with the infantry around, and the cavalry more in the center, and outside with four large corps of cavalry marked F.F.F.F.
	Serasker's tent with all the others from the Turks' Camp.
G.	

When the Imperial army marching in two lines with the baggage arrived on the right of Mount H. which contained the right wing of the Turkish entrenchment, the Albanian Infantry, which was there, fired a general discharge of musketry against the Imperials; but without doing them the slightest harm; and so that this post is well marked. I have designate it by the letters I.I.I.I.

The Albanians, seeing that this first fire had no effect, withdrew hastily to their entrenchments; and seeing that the Imperials were following them quickly, they tried to begin the new entrenchment K. K., but they were stopped by the Imperials, whose march is marked by dots, and was, according to their custom, in two lines, which ranged themselves in the plain L. L. L.

The Turks had barely seen the fire of the first line of the Imperials kill some of them, then they took the formation as it is marked by the letters M.M.M.M. This line was reinforced by some squadrons detached from the posts marked by points that show its movements.

Part of the Turks escaped by the stockade, and the small redoubt at Nissa N. to reach the bridge O. but the greater part threw themselves into the river to cross it by swimming, as one can see in the diagram. The river was swollen by the frequent rains, although the weather was very serene that day.

This entrenchment was very strong; the right wing of his army found itself covered by a mountain and the left by the Nissa River. However, it did nothing for them. The mountain that covered the right wing ended in a valley which I personally examined with 300 horse. I found it sufficient to defile the troops and to lead them behind the Turkish camp, and Prince Louis of Baden ordered the march. But the Turks, seeing themselves taken in the rear abandoned their entrenchments. They presented themselves in some disorder to the Imperial army, but be it be from the terror that they had of seeing their efforts made useless or by the great fire made by the Imperials, they were entirely routed, taking flight, and a great number threw themselves into the river, which was too high to ford, and they swam across.

The Grand Vizier Kiuperly, seeing that the Prince of Baden had retired from Semelin, where they were entrenched, attempted to cut off his supplies which were on the Danube. His project succeeded by a march which he made during the night and he took post on the hill a bit above Slankamen. He entrenched his forces on this hill which, with the Danube covered his right wing; and they joined to the left all the cavalry corps commanded by the Serasker Cimengies Pasha. The entrenchments were well filled with infantry; and the Vizier commanded them himself, as the Imperial army was commanded by Prince Louis. His Serene Highness began a small attack; but found a very vigorous resistance and lost many Germans, officers and generals, in it.

Marshal von Tinvold, who commanded the left wing of the cavalry arrived at this time within pistol shot of those of the Turks, but the Serasker took flight, without presenting the least resistance. The Janissaries seeing the cavalry fleeing to their camp also took flight and the Vizier, attempting to prevent this rout, lost his life in the attempt. One can see in this part of Plate XXVII and one can see by it the little valor of the Turkish cavalry and how the Vizier failed in his bold enterprise.

Plate XXVII

Explanation of Plate XXVII.

Plate XXX shows the plan of the Battle of Slankamen fought between the Emperor's army and that of the Turks, and the movements of these two armies, one ordered by His Highness, the Prince Louis of Baden, and the other by Achmet Pasha Köprülü, Grand Vizier.

This vizier seeing that the Imperial army had withdrawn from the sight of his entrenched camp, by Semelin, to go to the ruined Slankamen Castle, located on the banks of the Danube opposite the confluence of the Teise, where the boats loaded with provisions were located, decided to make a forced march in favor of the night, going a short distance up the Sava and making fire signals, to take control of the last part of the river, and seize, at the same time, boats loaded with the Imperials' provisions, and this project succeeded. The Imperial army found itself without bread, and the communication of the general magazine which was in Peterwaradein was cut, so it was necessary to appease hunger with the point of the sword. The Vizier delighted to see himself possessor of this last slope of the mountains, formed a camp there with some tents marked A.A., which he entrenched in the Turkish way by the entrenchments B.B.B., and he garnished these entrenchments with Janissaries, and other Turkish infantry, covering the left flank with the Danube, where he took, under his escort, all the boats of provisions marked C. with the exception of those, which were towed by galleys that descended the Danube to Belgrade, D.

Of all the cavalry, E., was entirely separated from the infantry; a large corps, was formed which contained the right wing of its entrenchment under the orders of Simengies Pasha Serasker.

The Vizier believed himself invincible in this position with the advantage of having his infantry entrenched, on the slope of this hill.

Prince Louis also separated his cavalry from the infantry, and formed two lines, which were placed in battle formation at F. F. F. F. out of the range of the Turkish cannons.

At the same time, he placed his baggage G.G.G.G. so that he covered his back on the Danube, and was behind the battle corps.

The smaller part of the baggage was on the edge of the river, and there was a battery H. to ward off the Turkish galleys I. I.

The baggage was guarded by squadrons of cavalry, K.K.K. who had the Foot Gardes du corps, L.L.L., with pickets, M.M.M.

Prince Louis of Baden, at the head of the infantry, being senior to Field Marshal Count von Tinewald, who was at the head of the cavalry, began to advance in a straight line, and consequently rather towards the Turkish entrenchment, and left his first post to move along the line of points.

Marshal von Tinewald, who had to make a circular movement, and consequently longer, with his cavalry to attack the Turks also left his post, when Prince Louis had started the attack with his infantry. The infantry endured for some time the fire from entrenchments before the diversion of the Imperial cavalry occurred; but having engaged the Turks, the Serasker barely defended himself against the first shock, and withdrew hastily, N.N. The Janissaries who noticed it, finding themselves uncovered in their entrenchments on their right flank also fled, O.O., thus, the German infantry entered the Turkish camp by the entrenchments, and the cavalry by the right wing of the same camp.

The Emperor's army was not as numerous as usual in the 1695 campaign. Marshal Count de Caprara[22], who commanded it, learned that the Vizier was thinking of attacking Peterwaradein and had entrenched himself in the vicinity of this fortress. In effect, the Vizier arrived with his army within sight of the Imperials, but he entrenched himself as well, and what had been unbelievable to that point, he began approaches towards the Turkish entrenchments. Count de Caprara was surprised with this novelty and

[22] Aeneas de Caprara (1631 – 1701)

found it proper to make another entrenchment further forward and to fill the area before it with mines, in front of the ditch, in order to obstruct the Vizier in his plans. In addition, the terrible rain that fell flooded the Turkish entrenchments, showing the Vizier his folly. He raised the siege during the night. The Vizier was unable to execute his plan, even though his army was twice as large as the Imperial army. See Plate XXXI. I am certain that one cannot help but laugh at such a bold plan.

Plate XXVIII

Explanation of Plate XXVIII.

This plate shows the plan of Peterwaradein, the entrenchments made by the Imperials commanded by Marshal Count de Caprara, the Turkish entrenchments, their camp, and the approaches they made to defeat the Imperial army according to the thoughts of the Vizier, who commanded the siege.

- A. Peterwaradein.
- B. The lower city.
- C. Two bridges erected by the Imperials over the Danube.
- D. Ships that covered the two bridges
- E. Small boats placed at a distance, above the bridges, where there were sentries to prevent the Turks from throwing trees into the river to be carried by the current and break the bridges.
- F. First entrenchment of the Imperials.
- G. Second entrenchment into which the army could retire.
- H. First Turkish line.
- I. Their second line, approaches and batteries.
- K. Ten of the largest galleys that the Turks ever had on the Danube and 60 other smaller ships and saiques.
- L. Two batteries on the little island in the middle of the Danube, called Klein-Waradein, to fire on the Emperor's ships which covered the bridges.
- M. Seven other Turkish galleys, which, supported by Battery N, harassed the flanks of the Imperial trenches.
- O. Imperial battery firing on the island and the Turkish galleys.
- P. Two other Imperial batteries that were not completed because of the rain.
- Q. Two Imperial batteries that obliged the Turkish brigands to retire and which fired on the flank of the Albanians in the Turkish camp.
- R. Advanced work to cover the post of Count de Marsigli, in a row.
- S. Two Imperial mortars.
- T. Turkish mortars.

The next year the Turks attempted to cross the Teisse to enter the Temiswar Plain, where they began to entrench themselves in the swamp using their baggage wagons, attached together, and with three men per wagon who were to guard, as I shall speak of it when I discuss the Turkish march process. This project succeeded well for them, and they wished to use it to cover their infantry at Zenta, which had not yet crossed the river as their cavalry had. This delay resulted from prudence and at the same time the celerity with which His Serene Highness Prince Eugene of Savoy marched his army. One sees the plan of this entrenchment and Eugene's march in Plate XXIX.

Plate XXIX.

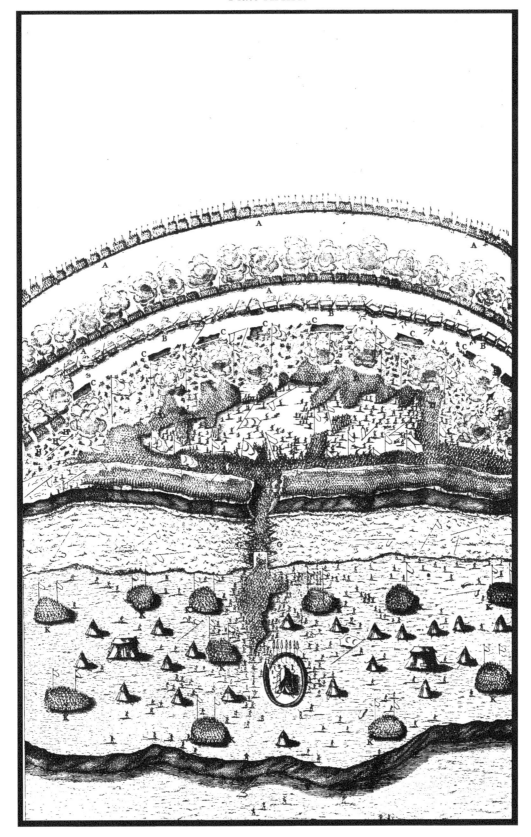

Explanation of Plate XXIX.

This plate shows the battle given between the Imperial army command by His Serene Highness the Prince Eugene of Savoy, and that of the Turks commanded by the Sultan Mustafa, their Emperor, who had the Grand Vizier with him.

The Turks seeing the bridge completed were impatient to enter Transylvania and crossed the Teisse with their cavalry.

Prince Eugene initially encouraged the Imperial army to withstand the fatigues of the long way he had to go, and arriving at the village of Zenta, he knew that he had been told the truth. He immediately arranged his army into two lines A.A.A.A. in ordinary battle formation; and the Turks, surprised by this, hurried to form an entrenchment of carriages B.B. and started another of earth behind, part of which is marked C.C.

The first line of the Imperials began to knock down the wagons. The Turks, in disorder, fled precipitously, D.D.D., to reach the only exit, E.E., made on the other side of the river marked F.F. and crossed the bridge, which because of the great weight and the precipitation with which the Turks ran over it, broke in the middle. It broke at point D.

This rout caused the greater part of the infantry to throw itself into the river, where it drowned or where it was shot down by the battalions H.H.H.H. and the cannon of the Imperials on the two flanks.

The Sultan, seeing the entire defeat of his troops from his tent, I., arranged himself in the middle of his camp with his cavalry divided in corps K., at dusk and quickly went with his cavalry to Temiswar, without the Grand Vizier, who was killed among the infantry, and without a single Janissary near him.

Such a brilliant victory opened the road to the imperials to take Bosnia and the capital of Serail and oblige the Porte to seek peace through the mediation of England and Holland, which was then concluded at the Congress of Karlowitz.

This is how the Turks undertake establishing their camps. Where they encamped, according to their ancient traditions, it was simply surrounded by lines of cavalry and covered by a vanguard and a rearguard, as they did at Vienna from the siege of Vienna to 1687, in the vicinity of Oseck; where they entrenched themselves, as they had at Oseck, and in the manner that I have just explained.

CHAPTER XXII.
Marches of the Ottoman Army

The march is nothing other than the movement of an Army educated in the art of war. I divide this movement into three, the first is that which the troops do in order to assemble at the rendezvous, either by coming by land, or by some sea route, as it happens for the junction of the militias of the Ottoman Empire who are in Asia and Europe. This march of soldiers, for the convenience they seek, and the little order they observe, is not a real army movement, like the third.

The second is this march called an "*alay*", which the pashas do when arriving at the camp marked for the rendezvous, to pass in review in front of the Serasker, the Grand Vizier, or the Sultan when he is there, what the Janissaries also do their own thing.

The third is a real military march; and it is that made by the army from the first camp that I discussed in the previous chapter. This is the beginning of the military marches; after leaving a camp, they march to make another, or they leave the first to return, after having attempted some expedition against the enemy.

I will successively explain these three kinds of marches, and I start with the first.

It was an inviolable law, that when the Sultan, or the Grand Vizier, were going on campaign, their beautiful tents were deployed, with seven or five ponytails, in the plains of Constantinople, and Adrianople, according to whether the Court is in one or the other of these Imperial residences. And publishing that the Pavilions of the Sultan, or those of the Grand Vizier were to be erected, the whole Empire was informed of the march of the Great Lord, or of the Vizier. As soon as these pavilions were erected, all the corps of troops, which were not yet marching, set to work, and those who were already marching were pressed to arrive, particularly those from Egypt, and Asia, which were very distant when the war was in Hungary. The various places of the route are marked along the coasts of the Sea of Marmara and the Archipelago, so that the troops take the Royal Way of Constantinople, from Adrianople, Philippopolis, Sophia, Nissa, and Belgrade; where was, in the time that the Empire flourished, the rendezvous for all the troops, except those of Hungary and Bosnia who gathered after having crossed the bridge at Osek, where there was the most considerable of the army. Kara Mustafa observed this when he went to besiege Vienna.

It does not seem useless to indicate the maritime skills of the Asian troops, to pass in Europe, and in which place they joined the Corps of the Army in the great march.

The pashas of Anatolia crossed the Bosporus at Scutari, where they had the convenience of the boats, and arrived in Europe by landing in uninhabited places. They set up camp outside the city which they kept on their left.

Those of Media began their journey straight from Gallipoli on boats, entered the Chersonese, and unless in a particular order, they left Adrianople on the right, going to Philippopolis, where they remained while waiting for the army corps, if it was behind; or hurrying to join it if it had already passed.

The infantry of Lower Anatolia, namely of Aleppo, Damascus and Egypt, embarked in the ports which were the closest, and came to disembark at Salonika. The cavalry, which was more numerous, and whose horses were difficult to embark, advanced overland, at least until near Gallipoli and passed to Philippopolis. I saw in Constantinople the Pasha of Aleppo with cavalry that was so well mounted, that the horses deserved to be painted.

The militia disembarked in Salonika used to pass by Sophia, or by the valley of the Vardar River, at the ends of Lower Albania, to encamp in the Nissa plain, where they were joined by the considerable body of Albanians descending from the high mountains of this province.

That of Bosnia used to pass the Sava to Prod and join the forces from Slavonia at the rendezvous, after having passed the long wooden bridges which are on the Osek Marsh.

The Valvode of Transylvania ordinarily crossed the Teisse with his tributary militia, on the bridge at Solnok and thence the Danube, and onto that at Pest.

Those from Moldavia and Wallachia passed from their provinces through the Iron Gates of the Danube and entered the plains of Temisvar. This was the march of the Tartars, by order of the Porte, so as not to make them cross Bulgaria, and Serbia, whose inhabitants had their retreats in the forests, for their families, and their herds. They all crossed the Danube on bridges around Belgrade.

I saw three of these marches in the time I was going from Adrianople to Belgrade with the Vizier Kiuperly; but they were without any military order, so I make no account of them among the marches; considering them only as simple journeys.

I now pass to the second kind of march called an "*alay,*" or ceremonial march.

This is done by all the corps as I have said. During the summer the pashas do them with great magnificence, especially when they come for the first time to the rendezvous camp. I saw many of these while I was encamped around Belgrade with the Grand Vizier Kiuperly. He was kind enough to pass them by my tent, and I fully satisfied my curiosity. I boasted a lot, with the Turks, who were with me, of the beauty of their horses, and certainly they deserved it; but I did not say a word about their armaments, and I could not help laughing at them. To this entertaining spectacle, the Turks added another barbarous one. In this they dragged the corpses of the Rascians who had been decapitated, and passed those who carried their heads, to throw them into the Sava. They were executed under the pretext of them having been subjects of the Porte who had revolted.

All this gives an idea of the majestic train of the pashas, who must have it as it is shown in Plate XXX.

Luigi Marsigli

Plate XXX

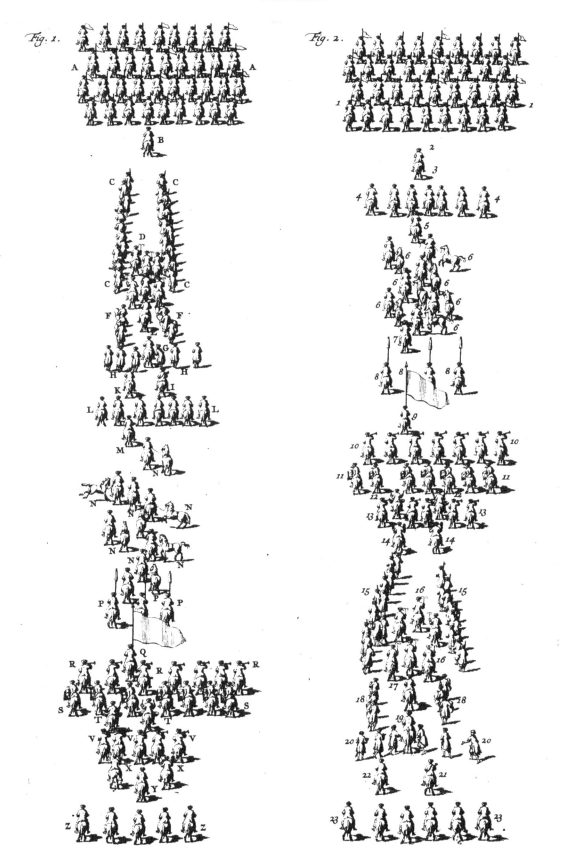

Explanation of Plate XXX.

First Figure
- A. Horsemen with their officers.
- B. Ali-Beg
- C. *Tuscgys*, or foot arquebusiers of the Pasha's Guard who number 24.
- D.D. Six mounted *chiaous* to carry the orders of the pasha.
- E. Mounted *Salam-Agasy*.
- F. Six-foot *gioardars* who carry the pasha's coats, pelisses, and other clothing.
- G. The pasha, who has six *satirs* to assist him when there are bad ways, and two who are always by his stirrup, marked H.
- I. A page who carries the saber called the "*selictar.*"
- K. The *asnadar* or the treasurer.
- L.L. Troop of all the *ichoglani*, or Pasha's pages. There were 20 of them.
- M. The *imbrohor* or squire.
- N. Rank of seven hand horses.
- O. Guardian of the Horse Tails.
- P. Three tail bearers.
- Q. Standard of the pasha.
- R. Seven chalumeau.[23]
- S. Seven drummers.
- T. Two tambourines.
- U. Five trumpeters.
- X. Two drummers with *chil* drums, discussed in military instruments.
- Y. *Chiaja*.
- Z. Several Agas.

---

[23] Translator: The chalumeau is a single-reed woodwind instrument of the late baroque and early classical eras. The chalumeau is a folk instrument that is the predecessor to the modern-day clarinet. It has a cylindrical bore with eight tone holes and a broad mouthpiece with a single heteroglot reed made of cane.

Second Figure
	Pasha's militia.
2	Ali-Beg
3	Pasha's Chiaja.
4	Agalary
5	*Imbroglio,* or squire.
6	Seven hand horses
7	Guardian of the Horse Tails.
8	Three horse tail bearers.
9	Great standard of the pasha.
10	Seven mounted chalumeaux players.
11	Mounted great drummers.
12	Two mounted tambourine players.
13	Five trumpets.
14	Two drummers with the *chil* drum.
15	Two ranks of arquebusiers, numbering 24 men.
16	Six *chiaous*.
17	Salam Aga, or Master of Ceremonies.
18	Six-foot *gioradars*.
19	The pasha.
20	Six *satirs*, two of which are by his stirrups.
21	The *Selictar* or Sword Bearer.
22	The *Asnadar* or Treasurer.
23	Troop of *ichoglans,* or pages, numbering 20.

The march of the pashas with two tails is the same, except that they have only one chalumeau, five drummers, two tambourine players, four trumpeters, two *chili*, five hand horses, and 12 arquebusiers.

By order and by the ceremony established, one sees in this plate the different orders of the militia and domestics of the pashas, the musical instruments that they have, and the posts where the horse tails and standards are carried. One also sees how the pashas march immediately behind their militia, placing the *kiaja* at the tail of the cortege. Some of them put themselves there, but then the *kiaja* takes the post immediately behind the militia.

The Serakuli Infantry, which is that of the pashas, on ceremonial occasions, marches by two, or four frontally, but in disorder, first after the cavalry, if it has not been raised by the pasha to join it to the corps of the other. As it is uncertain to find it with the pashas, I preferred not to give an illustration of it, believing the description is enough.

The Janissaries also sometimes make their *alay*, marching by twos, or fours at the same time, to pass in review particularly before the Sultan. Each *oda* or company, is preceded, or followed by its standard, and *giorbagy*, or captain, as we see in Plate XXXI.

The Ottoman Army 1683 to 1732

Plate XXXI

Explanation of Plate XXXI.

Plate XXXI represents the different march orders called "*alay*" for the Janissaries, when they arrive for the first time at the rendezvous location.

This march is performed in three fashions, represented by Figures 1, 2, and 3.

Figure 1.

The Janissaries march on a front of two men with the flag, A., at their rear.

Figure 2.

The company marches with a frontage of four men, having the flag, B., at the head, with the officers, C, the great flag of the aga of the Janissaries carried on horse at their rear. It is marked D, and there are two *chiagusi* of the rank of Janissary, to carry the *aga's*, orders.

Figure 3.

The Janissary Corps is divided into C. C. C. troops, each of which is made up of those of an *oda*, who have their flags at their head and mainly at the guard, where it is customary to call them that, whether the flag is of such an *oda*, or Vienna Company; and everyone from this company runs to join it. At the head of the entire Janissary Corps are several ranks of officers. The separate company, F., is the same as that marked E.; it is only distinguished by different letters to show the clothing with the hoods.

Finally, the Janissaries, in the solemn march called an *alay*, go on a frontage of two, or four; and on occasion as a troop, each troop is composed of a company, whose soldiers one after the other stand behind the entrenchments, or join together to make a large body of infantry.

I saw one of them in a line of twos, made up of 2,000 Janissaries from Cairo, when I was around Belgrade, with the Vizier Kiuperly. They were well-armed with muskets, which for weight, range and caliber were more like arquebuses, as I reported in the chapter on portable firearms.

We can say that Kara Mustafa's march to invest Vienna was an general *alay*, not only of the militia carrying arms; but servants of all kinds, baggage carts, and even the most abject merchants. He believed, thereby, to bring terror to Vienna, and at the same time cover the weakness of his army, having had banners placed on the most common carriages, and on the horns of animals, as I have reported in the chapter of flags.

Let us now see the third kind of movement which is the real one, which must bear the name of a military march.

This march looks at four kinds of things; infantry, cavalry, artillery, and baggage; which includes all of the militia's harnesses, the prince's provisions, and provisions and military supplies, like powder, balls, wicks, shovels and picks.

This kind of march does not always have its direction arranged in the same way; it changes according to the circumstances of the time, and of the places, as I will say below.

You should know here that the march is regulated by the Grand Vizier, or the Serasker by means of certain notes, because the Turks are not in the habit of giving verbal orders, except in matters of little consequence, or when time cannot allow it to be written. Besides, they use notes consigned to *chiaous* under the orders of the *chiaous-bascy*, to carry them where they are addressed. I had one of these notes being in Constantinople, I received it, from the same one who communicated to me the plan of the camp of the Grand Vizier Soleiman; and this note was one of those from Soleiman, who was chief of the largest army that the Turks had ever had in Hungary after that of Vienna; and I insert the translated contents of it at the end of this chapter. Reading this note, which carries the order of the Ottoman army's march, which is written by the Chancellor, who took it to the Vizier, to receive orders, will show not only what is the order of the march that Soleiman took; but still part of the way of getting started with the Turks; although, as I will say, they do not always work in the same order.

It is a maxim inviolably observed among the Turks, to make new bridges, on the rivers, and marshes, or to repair the old ones, and to level the causeways, to fill the ditches, and to cut the trees that would prevent, or which would delay passage. They also raise small pieces of soil, which they call "*unka*" every half league and even more frequently, especially in high places; and when the Sultan marches they raise two instead of one, as I said in the first part.

This army was very attentive when it marched and during the night, when it marched, they used pans of fire stoves attached to the end of a stake, which I described in the chapter on fire used for illumination. During the entire march, one heard neither drums, nor trumpets, nor timpani, except for a few strokes of the drumstick on the drums of the Grand Vizier that rarely occur, and which are accompanied by some salutes from the *Salam-Agasi* or Master of Ceremonies.

When they march in a friendly country the infantry usually precedes two or three days. It does not observe any order or company, half of the whole body, or even the same path; but it marches in a stampede. It rests where it wants, and arrives at the camp in complete disorder, and in platoons: However, it must be there, before the time marked for prayers.

The cavalry comes next; and although most often the general is at its head, it does not march with any more order. It even rests under the pretext of sparing the horses and takes little trouble to assure good order. This is also how the baggage, carried on carts, works; as well as beasts of burden.

When the army marches into an enemy country, it is a maxim not to separate the Infantry as a separate corps, and it is held together. One mixes the K*apikulu* with the *Serakuli*, however with this distinction, that each Janissary marches under his flag, and that each officer is in his company, so as to receive the orders of his chief.

They often divide the cavalry into two wings, and often also leave it in one body. Everyone marches under their standard, the *alay-beghs*, who receive orders, from the *chiaous*, are at the head of their squadrons, and the officers near the pasha.

They used to leave the baggage behind; but in the Hungarian plains, and during a few campaigns, where wagons were used a flying entrenchment, at the head of the Janissaries. This is not practiced for the Toprakli Cavalry, because having to carry supplies at its expense, it does not let them move as far as possible, which causes a lot of disorder.

They do not take the artillery away from the infantry either; however, when it is needed, it is still placed with the cavalry.

The march thus arranged, it was covered by the vanguard and the rearguard. The rearguard contained 4,000, 5,000, or 6,000 horse, the best in the army. It obeyed a chief named the *cialcagy-bascy*, whose employment lasts the whole campaign; and it is six, seven, and eight leagues ahead of the army. It withdraws in proportion as the enemy advances; and if there are Tartars in the army, or auxiliary troops of the rebels, they are made to precede the vanguard, because they run on all sides, plundering and ransacking everything where they pass. This was observed by the army which came to besiege Vienna; and then all the cavalry separated from the infantry, and did honor to their harnesses, weapons, standards, and other ornaments, which, as I have already said, could make the army terrible and majestic to the besieged.

According to custom the rearguard contains 1,000 horse. It closes the baggage and leads it to the camp before changing posts.

The Tartars, the Wallachians and the Moldavians, precede the vanguard, as I have said. When one sees that they are a large number together, a Turkish army is not far away, because the Tartars are never used against a Christian army, without their being supported by the Turks. General Veterani[24] experienced this. He was one of those who commanded the small detachment which, after the siege of Buda, was sent to take Segedin. In the strongest part of the siege, he was of the opinion at the camp that the Tartars, had posted themselves around Zenta on the Teise, to try to inconvenience the besiegers. On this belief, he detached as much cavalry as possible; and this detachment, which marched at night, surprised the Tartars, camped in fairly large numbers, as the spy had reported. The Imperials threw themselves on them with an unbelievable courage at the break of day and defeated them. The General Veterani knowing after this victory his cavalry was tired, he let it rest until two hours after daybreak, when his advanced guards brought him the news, that they saw the whole Turkish army marching at little more than a league away. There he held a great council on horseback, and it was resolved that, in spite of the few soldiers we had, we had to go out and meet this army, because by retreating into these vast plains, we would be infallibly lost. This resolution taken, and put into execution on the spot, the Vizier with his army of 30,000 men, in his flight abandoned his artillery and baggage to the victor. If word of the Turkish army's advance had arrived at the little camp which besieged Segedin, the siege would have been lifted; the Imperials not being able to resist the Vizier's entire army, still less to detach a little more than 2,000 horse. However, this resolution produced a signal victory, committing the victors to pursue the enemy, the only hope that there was being to be saved in such vast plains. We see by this way, and we prove what is the method which the Turks use, as I said, for their vanguard, which the Imperials did not then believe to be that of the whole army; but only a body of Tartars detached to inconvenience the besiegers.

This army, as I have said since the beginning of this chapter, was attentive enough in its marches, and very capable of making them longer than those of the Imperials. This was an effect of good food and of men and horses, which were better regulated than those of the Imperials, and which made them so robust and so fit to bear fatigue.

I will prove this detail in their marches with examples. In 1679 the Turkish army was encamped on the edge of the Morava River in Serbia, with a bridge on the river, and in front of Alagy-Isar. The Imperial army, which had a bridge over the same river, three leagues from the Danube, passed it to engage the Turks. It saw them advanced to Jagudin, where there were the arches of the fixed bridge they had there; and news came that the Turks were marching from their Alagy-Isar camp to Semendria, where all the Imperial food magazines were located. Count Tekely was only two days from their bridges, and advanced on the Danube side to encamp at Sagudin. The Imperial army suddenly found itself short of food and threatened with a revolt. However, they discovered the Turkish encamped at Patacin, just over a day from Jagudin, which shows the speed with which the Turks marched through the countryside. We can say that their marches were almost all masked. The Imperials thus seeing themselves without food and enveloped, as much by the rebels as by a body of the Turkish army, and being unable to cut their way out, made a bridge of small boats, which consisted of tree trunks dug out with a chisel, that the Rascian fishermen called a "*cianachi*." I myself was the author of this project; and notwithstanding that many laughed at it, I carried it out. Preceded by good guides, I transported myself to a place that the narrow bed of the river made convenient, and where the workers could be covered with cannon. In the space of a little

---

[24] Frederico Ambrosio Veterani

more than one night, by means of the wood that was taken from the surrounding villages, cutting down the abandoned houses, the bridge was completed. The success of this project pulled the army from the greatest danger it had ever been in. The Turks came, however, to appear before the Imperials, as I would say in their time, and lost the battle. This victory which was a particular favor of Heaven, through such an obvious danger, may well be attributed to the hasty march of the Turks who did not have time to recover.

In 1691, the Vizier Kiuperly, seeing that Prince Louis of Baden withdrew to the side of Slankamen, and as he abandoned Semelin, he decided to make one of these masked marches, for the reasons that I have mentioned earlier. During the night, he crossed the Sava at Metrovitz, then he crossed the Sarwisch, to reach the hills, and came to place his camp along the Danube. This camp was on eminences that were around the ruins of Slankamen. By this means, he cut off the supplies to the Imperialists, even defeating some regiments which came from Oseck to join the Imperial army. The Vizier directed his march during the night by fires; and as it was swift, Prince Louis of Baden was surprised and found himself obliged to fight a battle. This battle was followed by a resounding victory for the Imperials, however they lost far more men there than they had lost in any battle during such a long war. They reopened, with sword in hand, their communications with Peterwaradein, and recovered their food magazines.

In 1697 the Imperial army was encamped in the Basca Plains, in front of Peterwaradein, when Sultan Osman, at the head of his army, crossed the Teise below Titel, and erected a bridge of boats, which he had brought on carts. He had made a quick and false movement to the side of Temisvar, and he left it with the same speed, to rub shoulders with the Teise. By this means he left the Imperial army on his left for two days, to go to Zenta and threw his flying bridge over the Teisse there. He succeeded perfectly well in his plan and crossed the river at the head of his cavalry. However, Prince Eugene of Savoy, who was informed of this, notwithstanding that his army was very tired from a long march, and that it was very much suffering from a lack of water in the plains, because of the drought which reigned during the heat, precipitated his march and arrived sufficiently in time, to beat the Turkish infantry, which had not yet crossed the Teise, and took their baggage. On this occasion, he won an all the more important victory, since it ruined the Turks, as I will say in its time.

The Turks left their baggage behind, when they made these masked and precipitous marches. For example, when they came to Alagvisar, they left it on the Morava River. Coming to Slankemen, it stayed in Belgrade; and during the battle of Zenta, it remained in Pancioa.

Finally, to show what the march order of the Ottoman army, I enclose here the content of the note I promised.

NOTE CARRYING THE MARCH ORDER OF THE TURKS

Salie-Pasha Cialcagy, or Commander of the vanguard supported by Osman, Pasha of Sophia, and Delaver, Pasha of Anatolia, shall do his duty with all attention and bravery possible for the glory of our invincible Emperor Sultan Mahomet IV. He shall give the orders necessary to the Tartars, Moldavians, and Wallachians such that they shall discover the enemy and give prompt word of them.

Chiaous-Pasha, Serasker, with the pashas commanding under him, being Osman Pasha of Erzeran, Suleyman Pasha of Bosnia, and Mehmet Pasha of Temiswar, shall observe all good order and diligence which suits the Army's Guide and Chief of our invincible Emperor.

Jusuf Jeniser-Aga, with all the *odas* of the Janissaries, which belong to this Muslim army, for the glory and service of our invincible and Great Emperor, shall march immediately after Mehmet Pasha of Temiswar, with all good order necessary, recommending to the officers attention, bravery and good order.

Assan, Topey-Bascy, or Commander and Chief of the Artillery, with all your cannoneers and cannon and some munition wagons, shall march initially after the Janissaries and you shall take care during the march that nothing delays the march of your troop, which might give occasion to defeat.

Suleyman, Gebegy-Bascy, or Chief of the Munitioneers, with all your staff and the wagons loaded with ammunition, shall follow the artillery closely to furnish all that shall be necessary for the army against the infidels.

The foot *seimentys*, and all the other infantry corps of the provinces that shall find themselves together, shall observe good order and conform to their regulations, escorting the wagons of ammunition and in the need assist them to march with promptness.

Chiaous-Pasha, Serasker, shall take care to give all the *beglerbegs*, pashas, and *begs*, of the happy Empire and Blessed by God and our Prophet Mohammed, to march behind their infantry, and to assure that they observe the ordinary regulations and recommend to them attention and bravery.

The *spahilari-agasy*, chiefs of the cavalry, be they of the right wing or left wing, shall conform with our will during this march and follow the provincial cavalry, and hold themselves near Suleiman Pasha, the Grand Vizier, may God bless him.

The Grand Vizier, with all his court, the *teftardar pasha,* or treasurer, the Chief of the *Chiaous*, the *Reis-effendi* or Chancellor, and all the *agas* and volunteers.

Amurat, *Zairgy-Bascy,* shall follow with all the wagons of food, each of which shall have an escort of three men.

All the other baggage wagons and those which do not observe the required good order and disobey shall be punished by Jeghen Pasha Dondar, or the Commander of the Rearguard.

The same Jeghen Pasha, Commander of the Rear Guard, shall close the march of the army of our invincible Emperor, may God conserve it for the destruction of the infidels.

Janissary, 1657

CHAPTER XXIII
How the Ottoman Army Arranges Itself in Battle Formation

Here is undoubtedly the military operation of which the reader will be the most curious, since the Turks have been defeated almost every time during these last wars, when they gave battle to the Christians, either that they had attacked, or that they were forced to defend themselves against a great difference in success, if we go back to the time they laid the foundations of their empire on the ruins of the small remnants of that of the Greeks. They then subjugated many of the princes who had established themselves as sovereigns during the decline of this same Greek Empire. They won these two famous battles of which we have spoken, namely of Varna on the borders of Bulgaria, and that of Mohacs in the center of Hungary. These two victories acquired for them this reputation and spread among Christians this terror that our stories mention, and which their own historians have further increased. Unable to go into the details of the mistakes that the Turks make in the execution of the four parts of a battle, it is impossible for me to satisfy the reader fully on what he can expect concerning the military operation of which I speak. The battle includes four things, to know the disposition of the differently armed soldiers, to attack well, to defend oneself firmly and with order, and to make, if necessary, a favorable retreat.

As it is necessary that I speak of this with precaution, for very legitimate reasons, I will make a succinct description of the manner in which the Turks fought against the Imperials at the beginning of the war; and by this means those who know the military art will easily understand what caused the defeat of the Ottoman army.

I start with the Vienna campaign, reporting on everything that happened there, and which may have a place in this chapter; and successively I will talk about what happened during such a long and bloody war that lasted for 17 years.

I have already sufficiently shown what is the quality, nature, number and armament of all the militia orders that make up the Ottoman Army. It was these militias united in one or more army corps who fought during all this time; and one will be able to see easily, by remembering in the union of all these different bodies, with what difficulty the Turks can put to execution the four parts of a battle, while fighting against the Christians. In these occasions, the Imperials act uniformly, and on this uniform order depends the safety of our states when they fight a battle.

I saw, while I was a slave among the Turks, how they invested Vienna, and I admired the way they presented themselves in front of this fortress, which I have already described. They separated the cavalry, the infantry and the cannon, and appeared as if they had been arbiters of the campaign. The Grand Vizier, puffed up with pride to see that thousands of slaves were brought to him, which the Tartars had taken, believed that, without any hostility, he only had to appear before Vienna to be declared victorious. So, he hurried to present all the paraphernalia of his army, so that it was believed to be more numerous than it was.

Everyone knows that a camp, set up by provident and experienced generals, is an order of battle. However, that of the Turks was only a confused heap of tents and baggage, all placed in a crescent, according to their ancient customs. This order is not convenient for an army that is besieging a capital like Vienna, since any other than the Vizier who had formed this siege, would not doubt that a relief force would come. His camp was then in disorder; he did not know, nor could he oppose the relief force, in an order of battle that did not defend the approaches; and was obliged to seek its salvation in flight, as I will relate at the appropriate time.

He had in the disposition of his camp, only the essential foresight to keep the Janissaries at the approaches, by having the infantry camp at the beginning of these same approaches as close as the besieged and the field would allow. When the help of the Imperials, and of the Poles, whose glory cannot be disputed with King John Sobieski, began to appear near the approaches, terror spread among the Turks. The Vizier no sooner learned that this monarch commanded the relief force, than he called Ibrahim, Pasha of Buda, then only 24 years old, Dean of the Pashas of the Empire, and called the Father of the Militia. This pasha had always written to the Porte being in Buda against this great war; and notwithstanding the reproaches of the Grand Vizier, after the retirement of the Duke of Lorraine from the Raab. He protested against the siege of Vienna. As a punishment for this, he was condemned along with the Valvode of Transylvania to guard the bridges of the Raab, and to keep the Javarin garrison in check. The Vizier had him posted at the foot of the mountains, and saw that help would come; and, thus, gave him a command disproportionate to his age, which did not allow him to act in person, in order to have occasion to kill him in case he could not succeed in holding off the relief force. There was no one, during the three days preceding the arrival of the relief force, who dared to go out to go to forage, and to pick the grapes, as we had done the days before, because it was not far away beyond the mountains. Pride and presumption prevented the Vizier from thinking of changing the situation of his camp, entrenching it, and making the least arrangement that would have been made, and executed, by the least experienced captain. In such a conjuncture, he only excited the whispers of the Ottoman army, which could not suffer his greed, because he was the author of the tax imposed on the poor slaves, called the "*pingik*," which consisted in one sequin per head, which had to be paid by the one who bought them. He even tried to put it on the large number of slaves that the Tartars had in their camp; but they did not want to pay it; and almost rebelled. If he had not imposed this tax of which I have just spoken, when he saw that Vienna resisted longer than he had imagined; and supplies began to run out, he could have carried out the plan to behead all the slaves, who numbered several thousands and who consumed the provisions reserved for the army. However, this was impossible, because after having demanded the tax, the army would no doubt have rebelled against him.

The day before the deliverance of Vienna, the same Vizier advanced with the bulk of his army, on the side of Kolemberg; but he left his entrenchments in the same disposition as they were. The next morning one heard the cry in all his army, "*Giaur jachinder*," that is to say the "Infidels are close"; and a large part of the militia, instead of thinking of defending the camp, began to pack up what was most precious, an omen of what followed. I was encamped opposite the Soten Gate; and I saw that the Turks covered the edge of the mountain with their turbans, like a white carpet. I saw some go up in platoons, some advanced, and others withdrew. Finally, I suddenly saw them flee by the thousands; and even several of the Janissaries who were in the entrenchments, seeing themselves abandoned by those who were to support them, also withdrew, without entering the camp. I was completely satisfied to see Vienna delivered. I was detached from the stake to which I was attached, as a slave; and I was forced to flee barefoot, through the vineyards with the Turk who was my owner. I could not long resist the fatigue of such a journey; and I was put, to relieve myself, on a wicked nag that had been abandoned, and which happened to be on the road, and in about 23 hours I left Vienna alive. We walked all night in the moonlight; and in the morning we found ourselves on the banks of the Laita, where we stopped for lack of bridges to cross it. The Turks then thought of rallying the fugitive troops, who found themselves very numerous, the afternoon that we crossed the bridges of the Raab. I consoled myself for having seen, during the march, the proud fugitive Vizier with his right eye blindfolded, and despised by everyone.

After passing the Raab, the army began to encamp; but without tents because there was only one cavalry tent, which then served for the Grand Vizier. A false rumor spread around noon of the following day that the Imperial army was near; and this news made them flee again. The Vizier wishing to remedy this, sent more than 1,000 elite horse, to force the fugitives to return to order, and commanded the beheading of all those who refused to obey, so that in these plains, there was a second battle among the Turks themselves. However, after having the head of Ibrahim Pasha cut off in front of his tent, to whom he attributed this defeat, he put the rest in the ordinary battle formation. The Tartars advanced further towards the river, and behind the cavalry of the pashas and of the Porte; and the Vizier positioned himself in the middle of the infantry on the slope of the hillside covered with vines, which was opposite Savarin. We see this order of battle in Plate XXXII.

Plate XXXII.

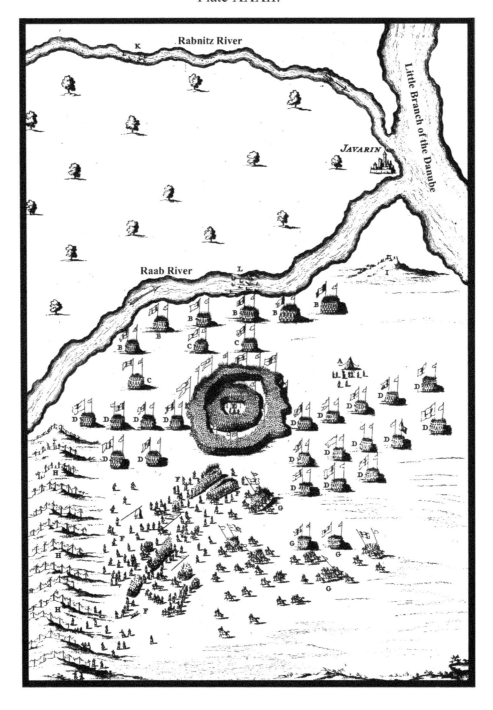

Luigi Marsigli

Explanation of Plate XXXII.

Plate XXXII shows the order of battle of the Ottoman army, which was routed before Vienna and which was defeated after having crossed the Rabnitz and the Raab Rivers, and where the bridges they had placed over these rivers before Javarin to besiege Vienna had been destroyed.

A. Only tent of the size of those of the simple *timariots*, which the Grand Vizier used for a day of rest, the army having suddenly taken flight, without stopping until this camp, where there were neither tents nor wagons.
B.B. Tartar corps posted along the Raab, near the locations where they had erected bridges.
C.C. Transylvanian Cavalry Corps.
D.D. Cavalry corps of the timariots, the zaims, and the pashas of the Empire.
E. Center of the Battle Corps made in a circle where the Grand Vizier was located in the middle of his court and the paid cavalry. This circle was surrounded by another formed by the advanced infantry.
F. Turkish corps, which, shaken by false alarms of the approaches of the Christians, took flight. The Vizier, seeking to stop them, detached some cavalry corps, G., to oblige them to return on their steps; those who refused were decapitated immediately, such that there was a veritable melee among them. I had the pleasure, although enchained, of seeing this disorder. Ibrahim Pasha was strangled at point I.
I. Mountain of the sinister justices.
K. Double bridges over the Rabnitz which the Turks had erected to advance on Vienna and which were then ruined after the flight of their armies, as well as the other two at L, which were erected over the Raab River.

The Turks fled into the woods during the night; and there was among them the man to whom I was a slave. We passed Buda through the woods, and then the Drava, without my being able to see anything more of this campaign.

In the 1684 campaign, the Duke of Lorraine having driven the Turks out of Vazzen, and a few leagues below in the vicinity of Bule, resolved to attack their army, which was encamped in the vicinity of Ergin, situated on the banks of the Danube. The Turks anticipated him and made use of all their cavalry, which, divided into several corps, dashed impetuously against the Imperial army, and made the last efforts against its flanks; but a shock so badly directed, and so violent, accompanied by their ordinary cries of "Allah Allah!", was repelled by the controlled fire of the Imperials, which forced them to flee in disorder on the side of the Janissaries. The Janissaries, seeing the rout of the cavalry, immediately took flight; and abandoned the camp, artillery, and baggage. This battle did not make the siege of Buda successful as two weeks later, the Turks returned to the countryside, fairly well supplied with tents, who gave continual alarms to the besiegers, and cut them off from their fodder.

In the campaign of 1685, the Serasker, Seitan Ibrahim Pasha, who had defended Buda the previous year, besieged Strigonia. At that time the Imperials attacked Naitel where the Duke of Lorraine detached most of the army, and crossing the Danube at Gomorre, approached the Seraskier. The latter thought it would be beneficial to raise the siege of Strigonia, and to meet the Imperials. There was a battle at two places in this area, which consisted on the side of the Turks, of howls and the shock of cavalry, saber in hand, always charging the flanks of the Germans as usual; but the Germans, who never broke, with a continuous and relentless fire, obliged them to flee pell-mell with the infantry, abandoning at their camp the cannons, ammunition, and the provisions.

In 1686 the Imperial army invested Buda on 1 June. The Imperial camp was very well organized; it was better entrenched than during the siege of 1684; and it opened the trench to form two attacks. The great Vizier Suleiman Pasha appeared sometime after with a powerful and elite army; he was looking for a way to relieve the garrison and spared no care or expense. He succeeded only once in throwing a few hundred Tartars into it; but he could never come to a battle with the besiegers, who were well covered by their lines of circumvallation. It is true that he did what he could to tire them out and cut them off from gathering fodder for their horses; however, he was finally witness to the surrender of the city, which the Imperials carried by a general assault, which was given in this way. The Imperial army was divided, one corps stormed the city, and the other was drawn up in battle formation behind the lines, firing its cannon against the Vizier's army. He was shooting at them, like the besieged on the besiegers, who, at that moment, discovered a battery, which had always been hidden, and which was used for the assault with great success. Such violent fire was made at the same time by all sides is memorable to posterity. The Grand Vizier no longer seeing the fire of the besieged, knew that the city had surrendered, and withdrew towards Osek. Having received news that Segedin was under attack, he resolved to go and rescue it with a vanguard made up of all the Tartars, and an army of 30,000 men, both infantry and cavalry. This army, as I said when speaking of the vanguard of the Tartars, was routed by a little more than 2,000 German horse, commanded by the General Veterani. The Turks, without getting into battle, took flight, and abandoned their artillery and baggage.

In the campaign of 1687, the same Vizier Suleiman Pasha, who had spent the winter in Belgrade to provide the means to set up a formidable army, came to an end and the Ottoman army was more numerous, than it did had since been that which besieged Vienna. Duke Charles of Lorraine, impatient to come to blows with such a flourishing enemy army, crossed the Drava a few leagues above Osek, and surprised the Vizier, not only encamped, but even entrenched in the vicinity of Osek, which had hitherto been unbelievable among the Turks. This entrenchment was done in the way indicated in the section on entrenched camps. Just and wise reasons compelled him to make this retreat, demonstrated in Plate XXXII; and the main reason was to protect his supplies, as well as the bridge over the Sava. He withdrew in their presence in order of battle, without their detachments, of more than 1,000 horses each, being able to do him the least damage. The Turks first took this retreat for a flight as a result of seeing their entrenchments abandoned; however, the Duke of Lorraine crossed the Drave again, and marched towards Ciclos to reach the provisions magazine, which was at Mohacs. As he found himself at the foot of Mount Arsan, at the edge of certain dry marshes, formed by the waters of the Danube, and partly by those of the Drava, he was warned that the Vizier had passed beyond the Osek Swamp and encamped with much advantage in the territory of Darda, as I showed in the chapter on encampments, with Plate XXIV. On such a notice, the Duke of Lorraine detached me with 200 dragoons, to march towards Ciclos, with the purpose of going there to lodge with the whole army, or to send a large detachment to cover the retreat he made. I was not a league from the army, before I received orders to return to the camp, which was in these dry marshes, and among the woods, enveloped by the Grand Vizier camped with the Turkish army; and I joined the Imperials half an hour before the battle. The Duke of Lorraine was on the right, and the Duke of Bavaria on the left; and they attacked the Turks without losing time, who had already begun to entrench themselves, in the paths through the woods, as we have seen in the plate. The Turkish cavalry, and infantry aided by the trees, which covered it in some way, made some resistance; but finally, it fled in disorder, abandoning their camp, which was very beautiful, their artillery, and all kinds of food. This was the happiest battle for Christianity, the most advantageous at home in Austria and the most fatal to the dignity of the Sultan, who survived this rout. Dependent on the militia, as it will always be in the future. This victory saved Buda, as I have already said, which still had all the breaches open; maintained the blockade of a number of fortresses near Hungary, and subdued Transylvania.

As for the following campaign of 1688, we no longer speak of the borders of Belgrade, nor of the Vizier, nor of another Serasker, nor even of the new Sultan Suleyman; but of the famous Asian thief, named Jeghen Pasha, who, as I have reported, had made himself formidable in the provinces of Asia by his assassinations. The latter, and Rustam Pasha, with whom he had taken Agria by starvation the previous winter, tried to assemble as many troops as they could, and even ventured to prevent the Elector of Bavaria, who commanded the Imperial army, from crossing the Sava; but the great fire of the Elector's artillery made them desist from their enterprise, and the bridge, which they had built, served to the Imperials to cross the river and go to invest Belgrade, which was soon taken by storm by the Elector himself.

In 1689 Prince Louis of Baden, who commanded the Imperial army, fought the Turks three times. The first was that of Patacin, where the Turks were surprised by the unexpected passage of the Imperials over the Morava River. It was at this battle that the Turks showed more order than they had yet made; by attacking the Imperials, they locked up their cavalry in a small plain, which was in the middle of the woods. They filled the woods, and the flanks with Janissaries, who were supported fairly well by their continual fire the impetuous shock of the cavalry, which attacked the first line of the Imperial army. Finally, several Turks armed with axes, tried to break through the chevaux de frise. As one was killed, he was replaced by another armed with an ax, in spite of the continual fire of musketry, and artillery of the Imperials. However, the cavalry seeing its efforts useless, withdrew, the Janissaries abandoned the posts of the woods, and all together they fled, leaving, according to their custom, artillery, ammunition, and tents. Prince Louis of Baden having made several necessary arrangements and knowing that the Ottoman Army had rallied again around Nissa, had a flying bridge thrown over the Morava River, in the place where were located the piles of the bridge, which the Turks had made earlier. He marched three days with great vivacity, and arrived in the Nissa plain, on the edge of the river which bears its name. The next day, with the rising sun, the Prince began to reconnoiter the Turkish camp, commanded by Arat Pasha, which was entrenched in the manner seen in Plate XXXIII.

The Ottoman Army 1683 to 1732

Plate XXXIII.

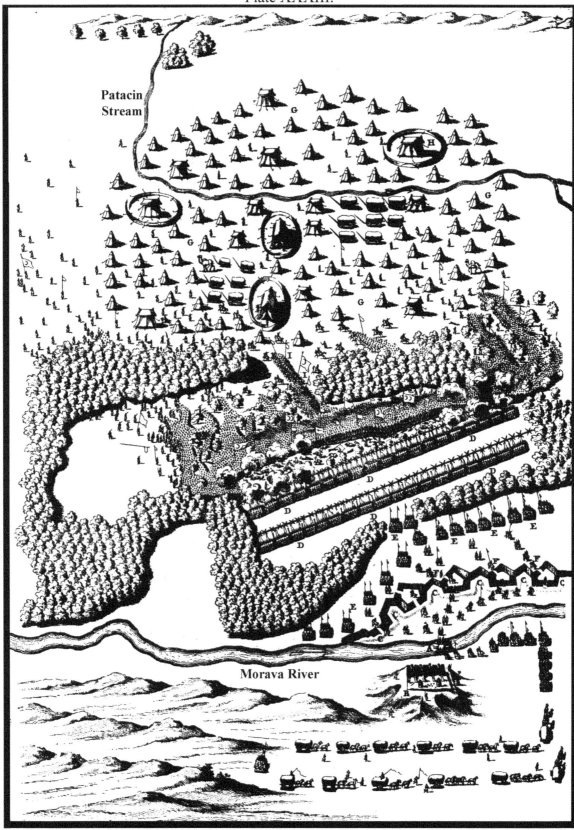

Explanation of Plate XXXIII.

This plate represents the passage of the Morava River, by the Imperial army commanded by Prince Louis of Baden in little boats made by hollowed-out tree trunks to reach Semendria. The Serasker Arat Pasha wished to cut them off and he had, to this end, crossed the river over a bridge which he had erected a few leagues above them. One can also see in this plate the order of battle that the German infantry observed after crossing the bridge to withstand the shock of the Turks, encamped in the Patacin plain on the great road to Belgrade.

- A. Bridge on the Morava over which the horsemen could pass first.
- B. Battery at the head of the bridge to cross it and cover the movement from a hill.
- C. Entrenchment that the Imperial infantry had hastily constructed after crossing the river.

It first took post in the Plains D.D., formed two lines in the middle of the woods, and covered itself with chevaux de frise. It remained under arms all night, while the cavalry crossed the bridge, and went into the space which is between the entrenchment and the wood.

The letters F. F. F. mark the march of the Imperial army on both sides of the river.

The Turks were encamped in the Patacin Valley, marked G.G.G. where Serasker Arat Pasha's tent was located, marked H.

The Turks wanted to take advantage of a fog that rose at daybreak and brought out all their cavalry through the I.I. to get to the meadow. The Janissaries placed themselves in the. flanks among the woods, K.K.K.K, and advanced to attack the German infantry. They first fired on it; but the Turkish cavalry not being able to break the first line of the Imperial infantry, they fled. The Janissaries who attacked the flanks soon did the same, and all the more when they noticed that the German cavalry had crossed the bridge pass and that it was passing through a hole made in the two lines of infantry. This hasty flight left the Imperialists in command of all the artillery; and they encamped there in their turn.

The Imperial army rested there for 15 days, to give time to stock up on provisions, and to build a solid bridge over the Morava at Jagudin with large boats. They wanted to cross the river and look for the Serasker below Nissa. However, the Seraskier had received from Sophia a reinforcement of troops, supplies, artillery, and baggage, which replaced his losses, and gave occasion for a second battle of Nissa.

The two flanks were covered, as has been said, the right by a steep hill, filled with Albanian infantry, and the left by the river, which at that time was very big, although it was not rainy in these countries. A similar situation aroused some fear, because the entrenchment was strong, and filled with infantry, behind which was all the cavalry arranged in order; but finally, by searching the Imperials found a valley at the foot of the mountain, in which were the Albanians, as it appears in Plate XXVII and that I was to reconnoiter myself, as I said. This valley opened the way to charge the rear of the Turkish entrenchments, and soon the victory was gained, by promptly marching the army in this valley. As soon as the Albanians became aware of the Imperial march, they began to form platoons. The rest of the Turkish army, who saw that their entrenchment were of no use to them, since leaving the valley, we were in their rear, without bothering to force the entrenchment, and instead of turning about and waiting firmly for us, they fled to the side of Nissa's bridge. Those who arrived there too late to pass, threw themselves into the water, where the greater part drowned; and we again captured their tents, artillery, and baggage; and the new Sultan who was at Sophia, was obliged after the loss of this battle, to retire to Adrianople. The Imperial army, master of venturing whatever it wished to do, was divided into two corps; one commanded by General Piccolomini, entered Lower Albania and penetrated to the borders of Greece, where he burned Scopia. The other, commanded by Prince Louis of Baden, turned to the Danube to besiege Vidin, where the Turks had, around this place, an army commanded by a particular serasker. This general, seeing the Imperials approaching, left his camp in disorder, and came to meet them. At the first shock, his cavalry which was repulsed by a few cannon volleys, fled to the side of the city where it rallied, to attack a body of Germans, who it saw at the rear of the camp seeking to loot it. Prince Louis and General Veterani arrived in the meantime and rescued the Imperials, who otherwise would have been cut to pieces, and the Turkish cavalry fled a second time on the side of Nicopoli, leaving weapons, baggage, artillery, and tents to the Imperials. There was a garrison of 1,000 men in the citadel, who surrendered two days later.

In 1690 nothing considerable happened, apart from what happened in Transylvania, where General Aisler got the upper hand over the Turks. Tekely's supporters also had some success, but the great inequality of the forces of the two parties was the cause of what happened the preceding winter in the Imperial camp in Albania, when a large force of Turks and Tartars attacked the quarters of the Imperial troops.

The defeat of General Aisler in Transylvania, engaged Prince Louis of Baden to go there with all his army; Serbia being entirely at the disposal of the Grand Vizier Kiuperly, but with no opportunity to come to blows.

The battle of Slankamen took place in 1691; it was bloody on the side of the Christians. The Vizier took up position in battle formation, separating the infantry, which were advantageously entrenched, as I have shown in Plate XXX, and enclosing his left by the Danube, and his right by all the cavalry separated from the infantry. Prince Louis was obliged to do the same, and put himself at the head of the infantry, while Marshal Tinwald commanded the cavalry. They attacked the Janissaries' entrenchment, who made a long and vigorous resistance, by a continual fire, because their cavalry did not break, until it was attacked by that of the Imperials, commanded by the Marshal von Tinwald. It fled at the first volley, and the Janissaries mingling with the horses did the same. The Vizier lost his life on this occasion, and the Imperials were masters of the battlefield, weapons, and baggage. If they had made the two attacks at the same time, they would have saved many people, because the Turkish cavalry, in the time that the German infantry would have started the attack on the entrenchment, would have also fled.

In the campaigns of 1692 and 1693 there was no battle, for lack of opportunity. In 1694, when Peterwaradein was besieged, there was also no battle; but only a 10-day cannonade on both sides, in the approaches and in the trenches. The two armies entrenched in front of the fortress, where they had erected their batteries, as it is marked on Plate XXXI. The Turks hoped to beat the Imperials by approaching their entrenchments by way of counter-trenches; but their efforts were useless; the Imperials were covered by double lines of circumvallation; and had a bridge over the Danube, under the cannon of the fortress, which guaranteed them a retreat if necessary.

There were no other battles in 1695 than that which the Sultan himself fought against General Veterani, who had under him only 6,000 men. Despite the unequal forces of the Imperial army, the Great Lord had much difficulty in taking advantage of this opportunity, even though he only had it, because General Veterani was unaware of the dispositions that had been made by the Imperial army.

In 1696 the Imperials wanted to try to approach Temisiwar. The Turks had started out differently from previous campaigns. We saw them in the middle of these vast plains which are beyond the Teise, covered by a flying entrenchment, made by baggage carts; and when the Imperials prepared themselves for the least action, the entrenchment was ready to serve as a defense, and the wagons were only tied together. However, the Elector of Saxony, who commanded the Imperials, suffered a check, and was unable to execute any of the projects he had formed for the campaign's operations. This shows clearly that it was wrong to spread the rumor that General Veterani had been unable to join the army.

The famous battle of Zenta, so bloody on the side of the Turks, occurred in 1697 The Turkish cavalry had passed the Teise with the Sultan at the head; but no Janissaries or infantry officers, not even the Vizier, had yet advanced. There was no other way for a retreat than this narrow flying bridge, which broke under the tumultuous impetuosity of the fugitives, so that the Turks perished, either by the continual fire of the Imperialists, or by being drowned in the Teise, which would not have happened, if they had the means to flee to another side. In 1698 there was no battle; and preparations were made on both sides for the Congress of Karlowitz to negotiate a peace.

We have been able to see by the enumeration of all these battles between the Imperialists and the Turks, often commanded by their sultan in person, the confusion with which they arranged their battle formation, and with what ill-concerted impetuosity they attacked the Christians. They never had any other retreat process than a shameful flight, after which they rallied and formed new camps, provided with tents, which they must have been supported by terrible magazines. If they had acted otherwise, the loss of their tents, artillery, and baggage would have resulted in the loss of all their militia; and this for reasons that I am obliged to pass over in silence. Finally, the general who will command the Imperial army will always be successful, even though his army knows that it is half as numerous as that of the Turks. The good order, and the firmness of his troops already accustomed to the howls of the Turks, and to their abrupt manner of attacking with sabers in the hand, will make him win the battle, which the Turks can never do. During this long war, their only successes was limited to the defeat of General Veterani in Lugos, and General Aisler in Transylvania; and again as I reported, with what benefits, and how did it happen? If the Turks who won both the battles of Verna and that of Mohacs had to deal with troops similar to those of the Emperor, they would have been obliged to return from Europe to Asia; but they found, as I have said, armies much inferior to their own, composed of nations armed in their own way, and which fought in much the same way; thus, they had no trouble winning victories.

We can finally see, by the examples that I have just reported, the difference that there is between the Turks and the Christians in the four parts of a battle, which are the order of the troops of which the army is composed, the manner of attack, the firmness to sustain the shock, and the retirement in good order.

CHAPTER XXIV.
The Turkish Manner of Making a Siege

When the Turks began to extend the limits of their empire, the conquests of fortresses cost them almost nothing. The terror of their name had spread among their neighbors; several fortresses lacked defenses, some were dismantled, others very badly fortified; and the discord which reigned among the Christians, was the reason they seized many others. The Venetians resisted their efforts enough in the Isles of the Archipelago, and defended themselves for a long time, and very vigorously at Candia[Heraklion, Crete], under the orders of a Frenchman, Morosini.[25] This siege changed the old discipline of the Janissaries, and the Academy, where the main militia was trained to besiege fortresses; and they established another method, with which they besieged not only Candia; but still at the same time Naisel in Hungary, located on the edge of the Dniester, a fortress which belonged to the Emperor Leopold, as King of Hungary. They then laid siege to Kamieniec in Podolia, which belonged to the Republic of Poland, and that of Zegrin in Ukraine, where there was a Russian garrison. The Czar favored, at that time, the Cossacks, who inconvenienced the dependencies of Kamieniec and Bender by their raids; and who ravaged the Dnieper by their piracy, on the Black Sea, even to the Bosporus. Finally, they wanted to besiege Vienna in the same way, which was, however, defended by a good garrison of infantry, such as might demand its quality as the capital of the Empire. The Grand Vizier Kiuperly besieged Nissa again in this way in 1690, which had only been fortified the previous winter, having never been anything but a redoubt surrounded by palisades, which is called a "stockade"[26] in Hungary. We see the figure in Plate XXXVII. The same Vizier then began the siege of Belgrade in the same way. However, he only mastered it with a blow from the sky, since a bomb set fire to the powder magazine. Without this, all the inventions of art could not have taken this fortress, since the Ottoman army lacked food, and that at the end of October, the season is very advanced.

Plate XXXIV

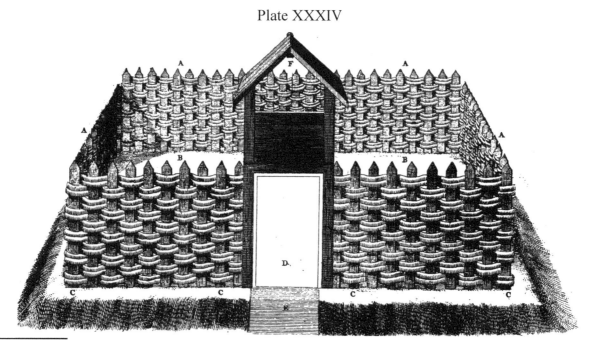

---

[25] Translator: For a detailed account of the siege of Candia, see, Nafziger, G.F., *Two Venetian Wars against the Turks 1645-1668 and 1686* (West Chester: OH, Nafziger Collection, 2016)

[26] Translator: The French word "*palanque*" was used, not the original Hungarian word.

Explanation of Plate XXXIV.

A.A.A.   Square palisade walls.
B.   Palisades made of round trees and pointed on top, planted in the ground a bit from each other to permit the weaving of the branches and thus making a sort of a wall, which they strengthened with mud.
C.C.   Ditch where the dirt is put behind the stockade.
D.   Gate which closes with a wooden swinging door.
E.   Drawbridge, which is raised at night by means of a rope.
F.   Small castle below the gate, made of wood, and which has a parapet around the four facades, made of planks, like G.G., with holes that form embrasures through which firearms could be used.

These palisades were sufficient to resist raids, but not cannon.

To show how the Turks besieged a fortress I will produce a plan of the attack on the St. Andrew Bastion at Candia [Heraklion], Crete] and part of the wall of Vienna, in order that one might see at a glance their old and new methods of attacking, without it being necessary to give a plan of other attacks. This plan is in Plate XXXV.

Plate XXXV

Explanation of Plate XXXV.

The first figure represents a part of the attacks during the siege of Candia [Heraklion, Crete], which were similar to those at Vienna.

The second figure represents a part of the siege of Vienna, the manner with which the Turks prepared their attacks, and for which one can look at the explanation for Plate XXXVI, whose letters refer to these.

The Turks will first reconnoiter a fortress, and then choose the most suitable place for an attack. At the siege of Vienna[27], this choice was made by the Vizier, who detached himself from the army with several pashas, and most of the most expert chiefs and officers of the Janissaries. They were escorted by a few thousand horse, commanded by Kara Mahomet Pasha, who, a few days before, had led the Tartars in the terrible raid which they made into Austria. When the Vizier had arrived within reach of the city, leaving several fairly advantageous posts, he chose this small height where the attack began; and batteries were placed to fire on the city. He then cast his eyes on the least of the exterior works which surrounded it, and on one of the least flanked bastions. These works seemed to him proper for the attack, which he meditated, although they were not the weakest.

As soon as the point of attack is chosen, they divide the siege operation into

> Soldiery
> Arms
> Pioneers
> Works

The soldiers should be composed, according to the regulations established by Suleyman the Great, of only Janissaries; but Candia's long resistance, which the Turks had never experienced before, forced the Porte to use the Toprakli Infantry, that is to say the provincial infantry. At the siege of Vienna, and even from the beginning, (which will doubtless surprise the reader, and which was the cause of the hasty flight of the army, as will be touched upon in parallel to the two parts of this work), the attacking force was strange collection of all kinds of cavalry, slaves, merchants, artisans, militias of all kinds, and especially Janissaries who were, and who are the best in the Turkish Infantry.

The Janissaries wanted to advance first, under the leadership of the officers of their *oda*. A company, which has entered the approaches does not leave it until all is known to be finished. However, they are only obliged to stay there for 40 days, as I said in the first part of this work, speaking of their statutes. Suleyman, who made these laws, did not at all think that this term would be too short if his successors wanted to besiege other fortresses than those of the Greeks, Bulgarians, Serbians and Hungarians. The Venetians made them know at Candia, and the Imperials in Vienna, where they felt the avarice of the Grand Vizier Kara Mustafa, and could not help complaining of his slowness, and the little gratification they received after the expiration of the 40 days they had spent in the approaches. They said that this minister was thinking of taking Vienna only to seize the treasures he supposed to be in this city.

With regard to arms, in addition to the portable ones, the Turks still use cannons and mortars, which they draw with buffaloes, oxen, horses and mules, as I reported in one of the previous chapters.

In addition to the pioneers who are given employment, and the sappers who work on batteries, or

---

[27] Translator: For a very detailed account of the siege of Vienna see Nafziger, G.F., *The Siege of Vienna 1683* (West Chester, OH: The Nafziger Collection, 2017).

somewhere else where their service is necessary, the Turks also used Sipahi, Zaims, and Timariots. These carry the fascines and gabions on foot, and even work in digging the trenches and the batteries, because, when the Janissaries had advanced the approaches enough during the night to cover themselves, they did not want to work more. It was, therefore, necessary to make up for it by other people, and to continue the other work necessary for a siege; and truly, if the Janissaries were forced to do so, it would be to impose too much on them, since they remained in the trench, as long as the siege lasted.

I will examine what regards approaches, both in the main, and in the casual, as the most essential part of siege operations. and we can have reference for these parts in Plate XXXVI.

Plate XXXVI.

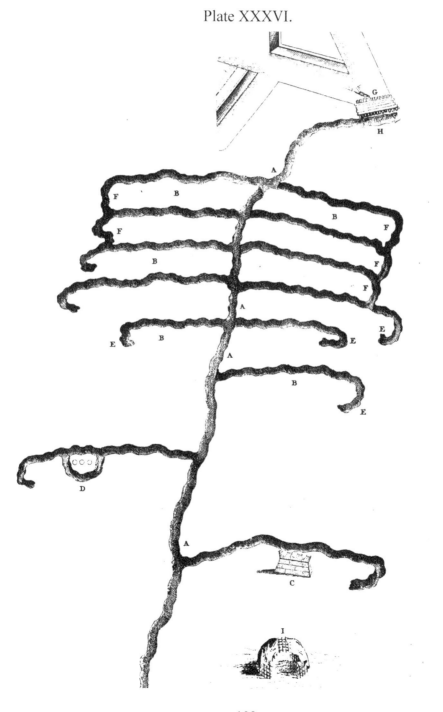

Explanation of Plate XXXVI.

This plate demonstrates all the parts that form a Turkish attack in a siege of a fortress.

A.A.A.A	*Sigian-jol* or communication trenches by all the following approaches.
B.B.B.	*Meteriz*.
C.	Cannon battery.
D.	Mortar battery.
E.E.E.E.	Musket battery.
F.F.F.	Liaison of all the batteries of musketeers, which the Turks began to make in approaching the fortress from the side, which made sorties easier.
H.	Caponiere or redoubt, called "*domus dame*," covered with beamsand earth to guarantee them from bombs and stones, made on the edge of the salient angle of the ditch against the glacis of the counterscarp, called the "*cobur*," and marked G. It is intended to descend into the ditch.
I.	*Koliba*, or barracks constructed of shrubs that are covered with a coat or other cloth to protect the soldiers against the sun and rain.

The approaches are ditches, the earth from which is thrown on the side of the fortress, to cover it from the enemy fire and the elevation of this earth, with what is dug, forms the trench. The main thing is to direct them well, that is to say, to avoid the string of batteries of the besieged. The Turks did not know how to prevent these inconveniences, for want of having better experienced people. The captains themselves wanted to be the directors of the works, and with a rod in hand, they imitate Christian engineers who use the fascine. They have, however, very little experience in these kinds of works, especially since the veterans, who had seen the siege of Candia, had died; so their approaches are almost always threaded. Besides this, the parapet of the works is not flattened, and even less are the ditches straight. They divide them in two types, under different names; one is called a "*meteriz*", or trench that goes near that in line parallel to the curtain wall of the bastion that is being attacked. And the other, which they call a "*sigian-jol*", that is to say, strictly speaking, the "mole's path", is that of a communication trench parallel to the previous one. We see the design in the plan of the Candia and Vienna attacks, where everyone can distinguish them. At the ends, on the sides of the approaches, they form a kind of semicircle, which we call "*crochets*"[28], and which they name "*joffek tabiesci*", or battery of muskets, with which they covered themselves. They are then joined during the day to later approaches, so that they contain all the attacks, on the flank, in a trench, which serves as a communication. They also try to make between the two approaches a kind of half-round, to cover it from enfilading fire. Indeed, nothing more disproportionate can be seen than these crooked approaches and of unequal depth, which only came from the lack of capable and experienced directors; that the Janissaries, who open them are not guided by a straight line of fascines, or by stakes;[29] and stand sideways, working fairly cross-legged. The instruments they use are fitted very short, and, therefore, proportionate, to the attitude of the workers. Besides, this way of digging enough is very advantageous for them, in view of the habit they have of staying in this situation, because by this means, they were soon under cover from bullets, and did not waste time to put themselves in a position

---

[28] Translator: A "*crochet*" is French for "hook", and it was literally a hook that swung back, away from the fortress and allowed soldiers to face to the flank, while remaining under cover to defend against a sortie.

[29] Translator: In the West, the trench was opened after dark with the workers following a line laid out by engineers. They would start digging and the trench was, as a result, straight.

to fear nothing from the besieged. The cannon batteries then are completed to form the attack. The Turks began to use this during the siege of Candia and have continued since. However, they did not employ them, except to knock down the parapets of the besieged, although quite badly; and drew them up on the eminences, which are naturally found around a fortress, or which they build with the earth that they carried there. Their whole study consists in opening an entrance to the fortress, according to the method that they employed at Candia, I mean by using mines. They rarely advance the batteries in the approaches as we could see in the fortresses they besieged, because of the difficulty of moving the cannon forward, through so many ditches, and parapets of the approaches, which would require an infinity of bridges in the trenches, and that several parapets were flattened. So they leave the artillery with the batteries.

Mines are extensively used by the Turks; I wrote of how successful they were at Candia, (apparently Christian deserters from the garrison taught them how to use them, as I said, where I showed how they worked on them and hired them to continue them); I will say no more on this subject referring the reader to this chapter. I will only add here that their main way is to find a suitable place to start a gallery; they chose this same place, at the siege of Vienna for the attack, as the most convenient to be mined, because the weaker side of the fortress towards the Danube on the two flanks, would have exposed them to see their entrenchments flooded, because of the swamps.

The Turks divided their mines into two types, namely, lodgments and the gallery. The first is called "*domus dame*"; that is to say, the "pig's home"; this is what we call a "*caponnière*." The Venetians taught them to use it at the siege of Candia; and it is only an tunnel covered with a quantity of beams and earth, to protect it from bombs, grenades and stones. The gallery is called a "*cobur*"; it is covered and defended by a lodgment and placed in the covered way.

The casual works are those that the Janissaries construct themselves in the approaches according to their genius, and for their sole convenience, not being expanded during the siege, like the Christians do. These works are small shelters covered with rushes and branches, which they call "*koliba.*" We see them in the plate that addresses tents. They try to place these shelters near the edge of the trenches opposite each other, where they are safe, because they make holes there, to take cover from the rain, stones, and even, they think, bombs; but ours having much more strength than theirs these sheds that can hardly protect them. They construct them at the head of entrenchments, especially at the beginning of the attack for natural needs, and at the end of the approaches, or in the middle, they construct others, according to whether they see themselves as little exposed to enemy fire, as a place to eat. Their food is brought to them, company by company in large copper boilers. This is how it was done in front of Vienna, and these small convoys were escorted by their *ascys*, as well as the water for drinking and washing, that the *sakkas* took care to provide them. Besides, the vivandiers do not fail to carry tobacco, and coffee around the approaches.

While in these works the Janissaries, where their accommodation is fixed, had specific military regulations which they were obliged to observe; for example, to keep their weapons in good condition; and each was to be at his post, ready to take two or three steps to reach the parapet, and by this means to fire on the enemy; for the trenches are so deep, that with a simple bench, as is the Christian practice, the tallest man could not fire over the parapet. This depth is cause that at daybreak the approaches not being outside the range of the line of the besieged artillery, they cover them with beams. Besides this, each Janissary puts grass and small bags on the ground on the parapet so as to make a sort of embrasure to fire his musket and cover his head; their courage is increased by the thought that they cannot be seen by the enemy, which seems to them sufficient to defend themselves from enemy fire.

By this arrangement that the Janissaries take in the works, we can easily see that, when they have lost these small conveniences that they obtain to fire, they remain, so to speak, as in a well, without being able to use their muskets, and are exposed to the superiority of the fire of the garrison in sorties, with no other defense than their sabers. On the contrary if the besieged enter into the work, without being well-supported on the flanks and back, and without having workers who make their way across with the sap, overturning the parapets, and that the Turks having time to assemble, they would be to pieces. This is what happened to the French during the siege of Candia, who had come to the rescue of this city. Their courage and their greed for glory did not give them time, after the landing, to rest, either to examine the parapets of the besieged fortress, or to observe the way in which the Turkish works were pushed, as we see it in Plate XXXVIII; and consequently the sortie, so successful in the beginning, failed and this produced the surrender of the fortress to the Turks, from which peace ensued, which left, even to the Venetians in this kingdom, a rather considerable advantage .

Finally, it should be noted, that to cover more and more workers, to maintain themselves in the advanced posts, to direct those who fill the most exposed places during the assault and to have the convenience of extending and deepening the work of the Janissaries, pioneers and other workers, the Turks used to publish among the infantry that they needed many workers for approaches. They imply by this publication that those who will offer themselves, will be rewarded by the Prophet Mohammed, in addition to that they promise them one more Aspre per day in perpetuity. We then very often see 500 or 600 infantrymen detaching themselves from the army and forming a separate body. They fly a red standard, under the command of new officers, and offer to do what is asked of them. This detachment is called a "*sarden-gity*", that is to say, "*enfants perdu*" or "forlorn hope." The besieged should not think of launching a sortie against the Turks with few people. If they are strong enough, they examine beforehand, as best they can, the situation of the enemy's work; and that they are supported by a sufficient number of pioneers, who not only destroy the works after the attack, but also who facilitate it by filling in the works. The princes who have frontier fortresses on the side of the Turks must fortify them with a united enclosure, and spare neither care nor expense, not only to counter-mine the body of the fortress, but also the glacis of the counterscarpe, pushing those countermines as far forward as possible, in order to weaken the strength of the mines of the enemy and their works which are so in use among them, and which they push with great facility, that is to say by their habit of digging while seated , either by their natural force, or by their lavishness at that time towards the pioneers. Let these princes having few fortresses on that side; but keep them in good condition; and above all, I repeat, that the garrison be numerous enough to guarantee them from the impetuous assaults by the Turks, who, on these occasions do not spare the blood of their soldiers. The capture of Napoli from Romania is proof of this and will serve as an example to posterity. They made no difficulty in attacking this place in disorder, and on all sides, although the works were little advanced; and abruptly threatening, they made themselves masters of it.

CHAPTER XXIV.
How the Turks Defend Their Fortresses

The Turks having successfully pushed their conquests and extended the limits of their empire, until the siege of Vienna, did not think of the defense of the fortresses, which they took from time to time, in the thought that it was enough for their safety to be in the power of the Ottoman Empire. From there came the little consideration they made of the art of fortifying their cities, believing that it was enough to repair the breaches they might have made by taking them. The art of fortification includes that of defending a fortress well. The Turks, who, since the establishment of their empire as far as the siege of Vienna, had not had the occasion to make a true defense in any fortress, so they did not have to establish a manner of fortifying them. They began to defend themselves in 1683, against many sieges that they suffered until the Peace of Karlowitz. I will try to talk about it, according to what I saw of their fortifications, and what I experienced in the biggest defenses that they made at Naisel, Aude and Belgrade, places that were taken by assault, and whose garrisons were put to the sword. I will first deal with their own old way of fortifying, based on what little I have seen and learned about it, and then some changes they made to Nissa, Vidin, and Belgrade, after the conquest of these cities. The old enclosure of these same fortresses had been constructed by the Greek emperors, and the Germans then added new works to them, which they maintained with great care, which they even increased. Thirdly, I will speak of the way in which the Turkish garrisons guard them day and night; and finally, with what works they defended themselves in these last three great sieges, until the general assault by the Imperials.

The Turks learned nothing about the art of fortification, from these ancient Tartars to whom they owe their origin. They began to take them in the conquest of Anatolia which made them masters of so many fortresses built by the emperors of Constantinople and flanked by towers both round and square. It is in this mode that the Grand Vizier Kiuperly, during the siege of Candia, built the new castles along the Dardanelles, to cover the old fortifications, which ran a great risk of being taken, and then were taken in the great victory, won by the Venetian fleet. The figure of these new castles was a regular parallelogram, flanked by round towers at the four angles. On the curtain wall that looked towards the sea, both from the castles on the European shore and those on the Asian shore, there is a battery on the waters' edge, of 16 large cannons; and we see in these castles redoubts in the form of keeps. These new castles were built on the model of the old ones which were at the two narrowest points of the strait. The balls of the batteries of the latter cross, when fully charged, which did not happen with respect to the new ones, whose batteries hardly inconvenience enemy vessels. Not knowing whether the old ones were built by the Greeks, or by the Turks, I cannot assure that the new ones are in the taste of one nation, rather than another; however, the keep of the new forts on the European shore, which are fairly regular, make me conjecture that they were both built in Greek style.

Being in Constantinople in 1680, I had occasion to have the plan of all the forts which the Turks had built in the islands in the Dnieper, after the conquest, and the demolition of Zegrin, as I have already reported; to prevent Cossack raids on the Black Sea. These forts are square and the angles are flanked by towers, with several faces, as seen in Plate XXXVII.

Plate XXXVII.

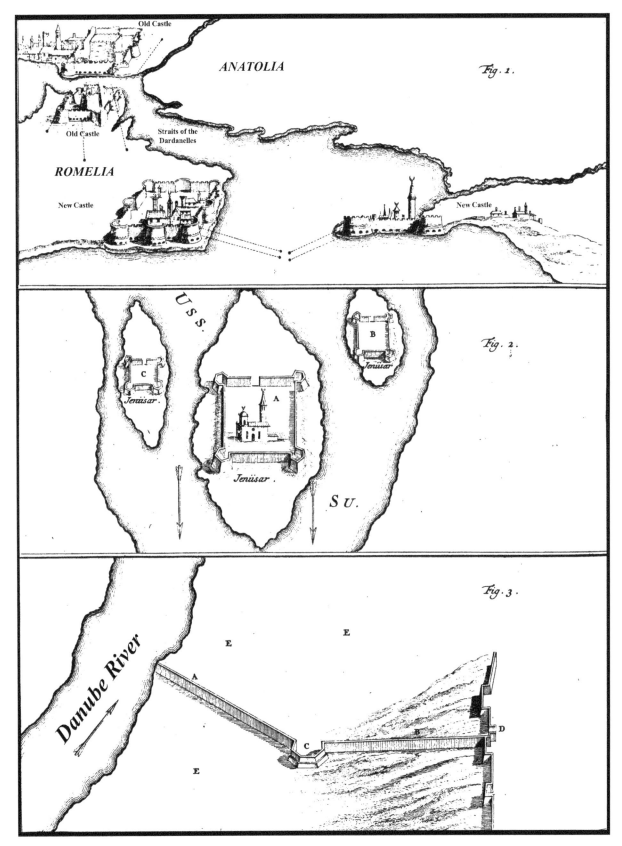

Luigi Marsigli

Explanation of Plate XXXVII.

The fortifications built according to the old methods of the Turks, constructed in the new castles of the Dardanelles during the siege of Candia and on the islands of the Dnieper after the signing of the Peace of Zegrin with the Czar, to prevent Cossack raids.

Figure 1.

The Straits of the Dardanelles fortified with two old castles.
A. The European castle.
B. The Asian castle.

The Grand Vizier Kiuperly, during the siege of Candia, had Castle C. constructed on the European side and D. on the Asian side, in the narrowest point of the Dardanelles.

Figure II.

The three forts of the Dnieper fortified with flanking towers A.B. and C.

Figure III.

Part of the upper city of Buda, from where the Turks draw a communication line to the Danube, which consisted of a wall without a terre-pleine[30] marked A.B. & defended by the tower C.
D. Gate of the upper city.
E. Lower city.

The first siege of Buda made by the Imperials, demonstrated to the Turks that it was important for them to have a covered communication path, from the upper to the lower town, to be able to get water safely from the Danube, that of the wells being all nitrous. The Porte approved the proposal made to it, and first sent one of the best Turkish engineers to work on this communication. The latter made the way and flanked it in the middle of a multi-faced tower, almost similar to those of the forts of the Dnieper; and by this means, during the second siege, water was drawn from the Danube protected from all insult, instead of being done only during the night as it was during the first.

We can conclude from what I have reported; that the Turks had no other way of fortifying until 1666, than to flank the angles of their round towers, or facing.

It is now appropriate to speak here of the way in which the Turks fortified their stockades in Hungary, which were built with stakes of very hard wood, planted well into the ground, pointed at the end and interleaved with branches, as we see in Plate XXXVII. There was most often no land behind these stockades; and they would then make holes through this rampart of wood to fire musketry against the besiegers, when they had ground behind them. They are flanked on the angles with a tower, built with piles as I reported. These towers were then filled with earth, and a battery of one or two cannon was erected on it, and then they called the stockade a "*kalai*", that is to say, "fortress." We see the in Plate XLI. Canisa, Sìget and Temisvar, located in swamps, which had once been small stone castles built by the Hungarians, which were then fortified by the Turks in this style.

---

[30] Translator: A terreplein in fortifications is a horizontal superficies of the rampart, being between the interior talus and the banquette. It is on the terre-pleine that the garrison pass and repass; it is also when the passage of the rounds. Jamrs, C. *An Universal Military Dictionary* (London: T. Egerton, 1816), p.255.

Plate XXXVIII.

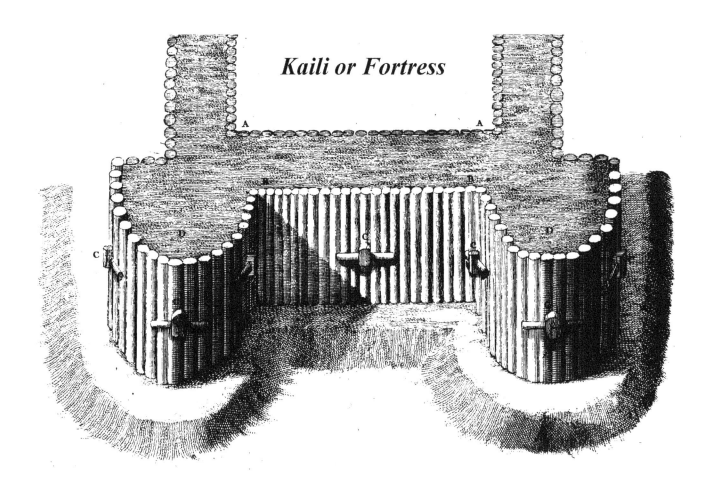

Explanation of Plate XXXVIII.

AA. Earthen curtain wall.
BB. Wooden curtain wall, half of which is constructed of perpendicular posts planted in the ground and the other which is put horizontally, attached with large wooden pegs marked C., which in the interior of the parapet, form a type of caisson.
CC. Tower that is almost round and which is made in a half circle, when one plants the posts perpendicularly.

Indeed, among these marshes, these palisades, thus linked with fascines, earth, and cross beams, are quite strong, and a cannon hardly makes a good breach. This way of fortifying is unique to the Turks, although many assert that they learned it from the Bulgarians, and others from the Hungarians; the latter say, however, that they learned it from the Turks. In fact, I know that we see similar works on the Trajan

Column, on which the conquests of this emperor in Dacia are in relief. But it does not matter to me that the Turks having invented these kinds of fortification, or not, and it suffices for me to report, that before they reveted their walls, they used the method that I have just reported, building their forts in squares or in parallelograms, and flanking them with round towers, or on the front.

When the Turks retook Belgrade, they found the parapet of the rampart much repaired, and outside with a finished covered way. The Imperials, returning to lay siege to it in 1693, found everything perfected and improved. The man named Cornaro, a native of Candia, who had served in this fortress as an engineer during the siege, had supervised these works. This officer had passed into the service of the Emperor, in the same capacity, and had been employed in Belgrade. When a bomb set fire to the powder magazine; and that the garrison fled while passing the Sava, he remained in the fortress, and announced that he had been made a slave by the Turks. He then served against the Emperor, obtained a large salary, and increased the city's fortifications, which he had built according to the true rules of the art of war. It was he who first taught the Turks, not only how to build the defenses, but also to push the works and revet the works. He had under his command several Greeks and Armenians who were well-educated, who perhaps still today work according to the precepts he left them. Besides, he was for mines, one of the best students of Chevalier Verneda, in Candia.

The fortresses formerly built under the Greek emperors, the Palankes, who had built fortresses, and the cities governed in the manner of the Christians, are guarded as I will report, and as the Turks practice in Hungary.

The Janissaries, as I said in the preliminary chapters, who are garrisoned in a fortress, have the custody of the keys, to open and close the gates, according to the laws and the statutes. They are reinforced there by detachments of Toprakli infantry; and especially Azaps, who have the most tiring jobs. The gates are opened at daybreak; and for that two or four Janissaries go to the gates, where there is a *capigy*, or doorman at each. They give him the key, so that he opens it himself in the presence of some Azaps. While performing this function, the *capigy* pronounces aloud a few words in praise of God and for the Sultan; and, as soon as the gate is opened, he gives the key back to the Janissaries, who take it back to where they store it. During the day, the Azapas and even some Janissaries stand guard at the door, and rarely ask the name of the those who pass through or where they are going. Shortly before dark, the keys are brought back in the same order; the *capigy* takes them by saying the same words as in the morning, in the presence of the Azaps and the Janissaries; and then hand them over to those who must keep them. The sentries of the fortress, who are all Azaps or Toprakli infantrymen, remain in the troop, because one must watch in the ordinary posts, while the other rests, in order to see if one does not attempt to do something at night. To observe if these sentinels do their duty, an officer makes the rounds; and the Turks call him the *kol*. This round starts at the guardhouse, and the chief has only a simple stick in his hand, with a corporal who carries the flag. Each sentry is obliged to watch over such posts and shouts "*Jegderallah*", that is to say, "God is Great." If the sentries, be it out of negligence, or if they are asleep, do not cry in time, they are put in prison, and they are given a caning. The director of these rounds receives an additional *aspre* per day during his lifetime. Besides, the Turks have no use of giving orders like us, neither in the fortresses, nor in the guards around their camps.

Their main maxim in defense of a fortress is to make a vigorous and well-ordered sortie. We saw the experience at Naisel, and at the two sieges of Buda. When the infantry made numerous sorties in the approaches, the cavalry which was around the fortress in the small plains, did not fail to assist it. They made no brilliant action at the siege of Belgrade, the garrison not being numerous, whereas at Naisel it was 10,000 elite men: and those of Buda, during the two sieges, of 30,000 and 40,000. Among this great number, during these last two sieges, there was the best frontier militia, which the Porte held dispersed in all the stockades, and the other small places in the vicinity, which were abandoned to reinforce the garrison of Buda; and we can say that this garrison was the flower of the frontier militia, and the nerve of the best Ottoman troops. It perished when the fortress fell by being put to the sword, as I will say below; and the Ottoman power thereby received a fatal blow.

During the siege of these two fortresses, whose garrisons formed an army corps, one cannot express the number of sorties they made almost every morning at daybreak, especially when they perceived that some flank of the approaches were badly covered or badly defended. They often entered it, saber in hand, howling; and they cut off the heads of the infantrymen, whose corpses they leaned against the parapets, and carried these heads to the pashas, so as to receive a reward of two sequins for each head. They took part in these sorties with so much valor, and so much haste, that one was often obliged to abandon the work that had been done during the night by day. The Imperials even withdrew in well-conditioned neighboring approaches, so as not to expose in an imperfect work the workers who had to perfect them the following night, by fortifying them with well-palisaded redoubts that were capable of resistance. The Imperials did this in order to stop the impetuosity of their siege operations. These vigorous sorties of 3,000 and 4,000 men, and the elite of the garrison, rewarded with an extraordinary amount from the public treasury, obliged the besiegers to push their work slowly, in order to have time to perfect and fortify them.

The artillery fire from the Turks greatly inconvenienced the Imperialists at the first siege of Buda, because it was far superior to their own; and the Turks suffered no damage from the bombs fired into the city, as happened in the following campaigns at other fortresses. At that time, the bombs not only dismounted their cannon, but it was still buried by their revolution, and consequently the fortresses were soon deprived of this defense.

At the sieges of Buda and Belgrade, the work that the Turks had done to resist the assault was cut, having been built with this haste which I will mention, speaking of the defense of these two fortresses. They did not do the least thing at the siege of Naisel, to second the disposition of the body of the fortress, which we hoped to find by assaulting two breaches, defended by a ditch full of very deep water, having only a narrow passage over two dikes of sandbags. There was a walkway at the head of the breach which, if it had been crossed by four beams attached to two cavaliers of the bastion, would have caused much blood to be shed, because we could not have climbed on these cavaliers[31] because of their glacis, and that besides, furnished with cannon fire, bombs and stones, they made an assault impossible. I experienced it myself, for, struck in the face of a stone thrown from the top of one of these cavaliers, I fell from the breach at the bottom of the ditch, which was full of water. We will see in the following plate all these difficulties, as well as the failure of the Turks to take advantage of the weaknesses that the fortifications provided them.

The Imperials made two attacks in the second siege of Buda. The main one which took the fortress, was under the orders of the Duke of Lorraine, on the side of the lower town, which destroyed the curtain wall with all the more facility, as it consisted only of a simple wall without a terreplein. The Turks, according to their maxim, that one must be covered to have more courage, made, as usual, deep ditches behind the breach, furnished with a palisaded parapet; but feeling that the Imperials were approaching to launch an assault, and finding themselves unable to resist them, they abandoned them. We see the design in Plate LIX.

---

[31] Translator: A cavalier is a work made under the rampart, like a cellar or cave, with loopholes to place cannon in it. James, C. *An Universal Military Dictionary* (London: T. Egerton, 1816.) p.248.

Plate LIX.

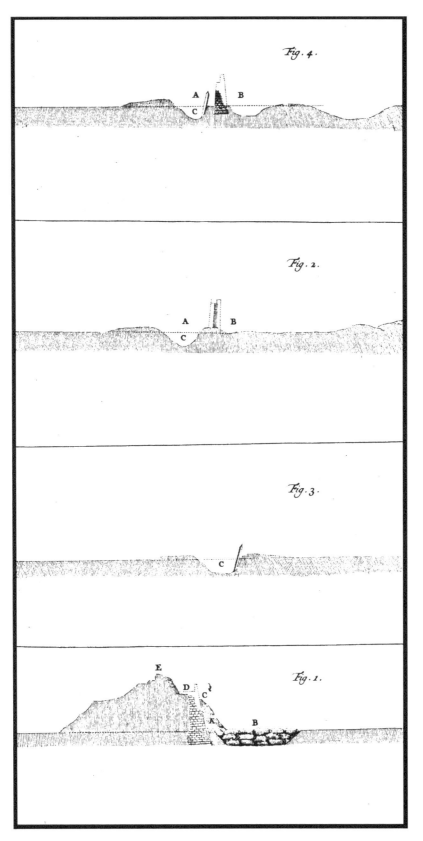

Explanation of Plate LIX.

Plate LXII shows the profiles of the breaches at Naisel and of the lower city of Buda, with the Turkish entrenchments.

Figure I.

A. Profile of the breach at Naisel.
B. Dike made in the ditch full of water with sandbags.
C. Breach at Naisel by which the Imperials mounted their assault.
D. Path of the rounds, which surrounded not only the cavalier, E., but also all the fortress, where the Imperials feared they would find obstacles, but the Turks did not profit from their advantages and left the cavaliers, which were taken in the fortress by the parapets of the curtain walls.

Figure II.

A. Profile of the lower city of Buda.
B. Wall behind the curtain wall, which formed a double rampart without a terreplein. There was a gallery of wood, by which the garrison made a tower.
C. Interior ditch constructed to serve as a retreat for the Turks, as you can see by Profile III. This so-called and ridiculous defense was behind the breach which the Imperials had made, as one can see in Profile IV. However, knowing it was incapable of a defense, they abandoned it quickly.

The upper city defended itself, as one can expect from an army, posted on a steep hill, covered with ramparts and furnished with artillery of every sort of munitions and expense and in such great quantities that there was sufficient for the defense of three cities. It must be added that courage inspired the garrison, at the sight of an army of 60,000 men, commanded by the Grand Vizier, who stood every day in the vicinity of Buda.

Sorties were the principal defense by the Turks during a siege. They took care to clean out, during the night, the ruins in the breaches that the Christian artillery had made during the day and to hold a small body of troops behind the breach which had been made by the Duke of Lorraine's attacking batteries. There was no solid rampart in this location as on the side of the attack being made by the Elector of Bavaria.

A precipitous assault was made against the lower city. The Turks seeing that the breach was not achieved and ho found themselves in a condition to defend it, the Janissaries executed a great carnage with sacks of powder. The Duke of Lorraine then enlarged the breach, bring up the artillery, and fire on the second wall, separated down that side, from the great tower, where there was a breach by the ditch, which was so narrow that two men could not pass abreast. The Turks, as was their practice, raised on the second rampart a parapet, with some caissons full of earth that were linked together and reinforced with beams that surrounded it like a palisade, as one can see in Plate XL.

Plate XL.

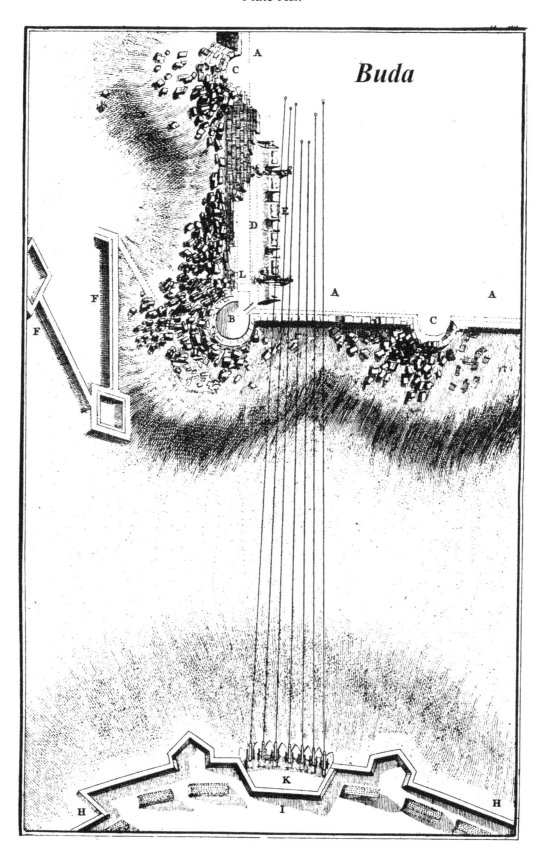

Explanation of Plate XL.

In this plate one sees the defenses and the entrenchment that the Turks made at Buda to oppose the attack of the Duke of Lorraine, who directed this siege.

A.A.A.	Part of the fortress.
B.	Tower where a breach was opened to launch the attack.
C.C.	Two towers that were beaten into ruins because they defended the breach.
D.	Interior rampart that the attackers did not see. It was separated from the curtain wall by a ditch.
E.	Entrenchment behind the second rampart, made with caissons filled with earth and attached by heavy beams. There was a palisaded parapet of sandbags as one can see better in the plate that represents the works the Turks made at Belgrade.
F.	Part of the Imperial approaches.
G.	Battery erected on planks, to try to beat the entrenchment E. which a bit in this place.
H.H.	Part of the line of circumvallation laid out on a hill, I., where the Swabian troops were encamped and which, for this reason, was named the "Swabian Hill," from where one could see the rear of the Turkish entrenchments E.
K.	Barrier established on the mountain and held covered until the moment of the assault and which, as one can judge from the plate, was then the cause of the capture of the fortress, whereas there was no other passage from tower B. on the ditch D. between two walls than one that was so tight, that only two men could pass abreast. When the Turks began to perceive the effect of the Swabian battery, they abandoned the entrenchment E. and left to the besiegers the small passage, L., entirely free, by which the Imperials launched their assault.

The open communication with the grand tower, where only two men could pass abreast, was deemed appropriate at noon to support the assault. The Duke of Lorraine called on me two hours before it began; and communicated to me that he was afraid of attempting to enter a fortress where the garrison was large enough to form an army; and having only such a narrow passage. All our hope was in the effect of the battery of 6 cannon, erected on the hill, called the "Swabian Hill," because the Swabian troops were encamped there, and that they were kept hidden from the Turks until the moment of the assault. They began to fire this battery, whose guns, pointed correctly, beat back the Turks, who defended the entrenchment, and who disputed the small passage of the ditch. Surprised by the fire from this battery which they did not expect, confusion arose among them, and they no longer had the courage to confront those who were assaulting them, commanded by Baron d'Asti, a Roman gentleman, who died on this occasion. The Turks then seeing themselves pressed on all sides, fled with haste towards the castle, and left the city in the hands of Imperials, who put the garrison to the sword. We see in the plate above what was the effect of this battery. The Imperials laid siege to Belgrade in 1688. As soon as the Turks saw them pass the Sava, they retired in disorder into the fortress, and fortified it according to their ordinary method, on the side of the Danube, in the manner seen in Plate XLIV.

Explanation of Plate XLI.

This plate demonstrates the defensive works made by the Turks at Belgrade in 1688, which the Imperials besieged.

A.A.	Part of the upper city of Belgrade
B.	Breach repaired with caissons, beams, palisades and sandbags, as one can see in Profile I. This made the breach look like what is shown at Profile II. There was a lodgment marked 3.3. at the foot of the breach where one sees the counterscarpe, 4., which was destroyed by mines, which made the lodgment useless.
C.	Entrenchment made with equal parts of caissons, palisades, and sandbags, which abutted the second rampart, D.D.
E.E.E.E.	Traverses that covered the gate, F., to go to the lower city by the passages from the upper countryside. These works were constructed as one can see by Figure 5, in Profile IV. To better cover the defense, they had dug a ditch in the middle marked 6., where the earth served to elevate the fortifications which they had palisaded obliquely, with sacks marked 7. 7., between each palisade.
	They had raised, in several locations, a parapet of sandbags with a palisade in front, as is marked in Profile III, by number 8.
G.	Grand battery organized to defend the gate F, which served for nothing, because it could not see the works, nor the Imperial's attack. The repairs of the breach, all the mentioned works, like the entrenchment C, and the other works were badly constructed and useless. The Germans mounted the assault and the Turks fled hastily into the citadel. A large number that could not get into it were put to the sword.
	Caissons that closed the breach, B.B., were constructed as those marked 9, in Profile IV, and were entirely similar to those that were used at Buda.

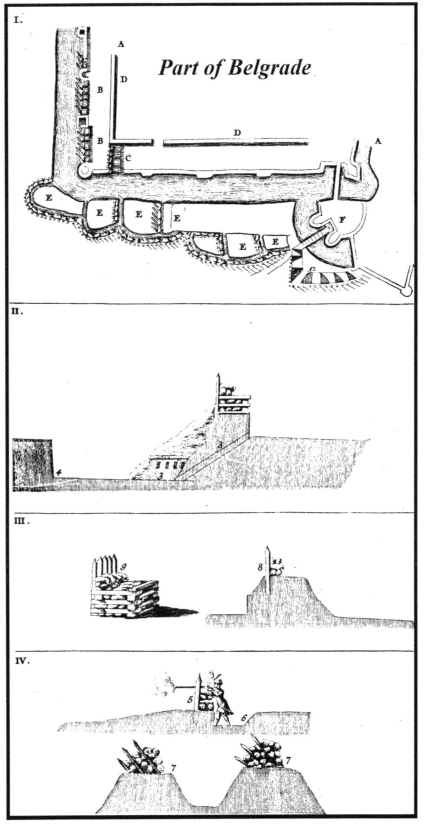

This plate still represents the situation of the attack, and the plan of a work which they had built a few months before, flanked very irregularly. The whole was raised with sandbags, beams, and palisades, as they had always practiced until then, not having yet learned the art of the fortifications, which were taught to them by renegade Christians. The breaches made by the Imperial batteries were barricaded by beams, sandbags, and palisades. They dug a trench behind it, which led to the rampart of the second enclosure; and made an lodgment at the foot of the breach, which they call a "*domus-dame*," as I said. But all these works were not very useful. The counterscarpe was ruined by mines, and the breach being large enough, the assault was made. No sooner did the Imperials appear than the Turks, without making the slightest resistance, abandoned the entrenchments, and fled hastily to the citadel. Those who could not get there in time, were put to the sword; and those who had retired to the citadel were made slaves. We see in the Plate XLIV the representation of all that I have just reported, with the replication, so that everyone can understand it, and their entrenchments, and their works, and their defensive fortification, on the model from what they practiced at Buda, and what they learned at Candia.

All their other principal Hungarian fortresses were starved into surrendering, with the exception of Gross-Waradein, whose garrison, although weakened by the lack of food, withstood a siege with an open trench. I was not there; but I was told of everything that happened. The Turks began there some works similar to those of which I mentioned, and which I will pass over in silence, saying only that this fortress surrendered by capitulation.

One can conceive by all that I have reported, the nature of Turkish defensive fortification, prior to the Peace of Karlowitz, from what I have said above all, by what I have seen from the principal sieges, where being pressed by the enemy, during the assaults, they were doing what they had been accustomed to in battles, I mean that they abandoned the entrenchments. The officers withdrew where they hoped to capitulate and save their lives; but this however did not succeed in Naisel, where they did not have the convenience of withdrawing as in Buda and Belgrade. Besides, their flight in sieges came from the same motive as their flight in battles.

Now, in the future, when we besiege some fortress defended by the Turks, that we must make good and big breaches, to mount a frontal assault, and in good order. The Turks finding themselves in a hurry will undoubtedly flee, as they have in the past.

TURKISH MILITARY OPERATIONS AT SEA

Chapter XXVI.
The Turkish Fleet

Turks came to settle in Asia, along the shores of the Sea of Marmara, from the birth of their Empire, and Burse in Bitinia, a day and a half distant from this sea, was chosen to be its capital. They saw themselves in a short time superior in maritime forces to Constantinople, the former capital of the Eastern Empire, and located in Europe on the opposite shore of the same sea. The thing would be incredible, if the events had left some place to doubt it, and if they had not shown that the wrath of Heaven, which, ruler of empires, allows the destruction of one for the enlargement of the other, was the first spring, which took them from Asia to Europe. Discord tore Christians apart; no one thought of defending the shores of the Sea of Marmara; and they were allowed to disembark. They first began to make establishments; and finally pushed their conquests the way everyone does. Sultan Mahomet II, descendant of Osman I, tried this passage several times, with some troops, and had a large number of ships made for this purpose. We do not know if this victorious sultan established a shipyard in Asia, on the same banks of the Sea of Marmara, so, instead of warships, he must have had only boats, whose construction may have been taught to them, and what some unfortunate Christians may have worked on, animated by the greed for gain and the hope of a better fate.

The *Canon-Name* does not mention any regulated Turkish naval armament of any size before the reign of Sultan Selim, called the "Old Man." This monarch, by the Council of the Grand Vizier Pery Pasha, had the shipyards built, as I said, for the construction of all kinds of ships, with oars, as they were in use among the Venetians; and built 500 ships, which the *Canon-Name* mentions. This great number of ships inspired, in the Republic of Venice, and in all of Christendom a just jealousy, which the victories of a formidable enemy produced. The laws for the establishment of the navy were then established in the Ottoman Empire; and they regulated the quantity, and the diversity of the woods and materials, which each province had to supply, which is written in the *Canon-Name*. We saw since that time every day something new for perfection, and advantage of the navy, until the year 1691, which was so fatal to the Turks, as I will say below.

The reader here expects, no doubt, that I treat the Turkish maritime operations, as I may have done those on land, albeit rather poorly; but I admit that I cannot speak of it, even in this way. I have never served at sea, neither against the Turks, nor against any other nation whatsoever; thus, this chapter will contain only what I saw in Constantinople of the navy of the Turks in 1679 and 1680. Very young, though I was, I forgot nothing, to satisfy my particular inclination to know the genius of the nation; and specially to consider what I am going to talk about. I tried to increase and then improve this knowledge during my stay there in 1692, time when my age had matured my judgment; and to which the job with which I was invested at the Porte gave me the opportunity to see many things.

I will clarify the following during these two different stays; and to bring these clarifications to light, I divide this chapter into three parts. I will show in the first place how I had occasion to examine it, and to judge that the Straits of the Dardanelles is not impregnable, as the Turks imagine it in the second place. I will describe the sortie that Sultan Mahomet IV had made to the fleet of all the shipyards, which he wanted to see at the point of the Seraglio; and whose meeting was at the Isles of Papassi, on the Sea of Marmara, 18 miles from Constantinople. Thirdly, I will report that whenever I went to the seaside, I saw warships built, in the most exact proportions, which would have been kept by the most experienced maritime Christian nations. The construction of these ships was directed by Christians, dressed in the

European style, who, with cane in hand, directed the workers by means of the interpreters.

With regard to the first chief, I will be a bit verbose, not because of what I have to say concerning the Straits of the Dardanelles, but because I am very happy to take this opportunity to express my gratitude to two senators of the Republic of Venice, to whom I owe everything on this subject.

The new Baile[32], Pierre Ciurani, Senator of the Republic of Venice, a man of perfect integrity, and consummate prudence, and known to the whole nation, came to Constantinople to relieve the Cavaliere[33] Jean Morosini Procurator, who had completed the time of his ministry. No sooner had he arrived than the Grand Vizier Kara Mustafa Pasha, of whom I have spoken so often, with the help of the Director of the Customs of Constantinople, wanted to make room for him. This vizier claimed that there was a large quantity of golden cloth on the ships which had brought to the Baile; and that these goods paying no duty, the Treasury of the Sultan suffered greatly. He wanted to be presented with several purses of money; and threatened to confiscate, in the event of refusal, all the goods that the Venetians had in their warehouses, which would be seized. Nothing would dissuade the Vizier from his claims, although according to the custom, one protested on the contrary. It was only a pretext to impose a tribute on all the nations that traded with Constantinople, with the only difference being more or less: also, to save the funds which the Christians had in Turkey, so the Venetians resolved to satisfy the greed of these people, all with as little expense as possible. The Baile Ciurani entered; the Grand Vizier gave him an audience, and the Procurator Morasini, with the usual ceremonies, and all the ambassadors of the Christian powers attended. Procurator Morosini, attacked by gout, and besides suffering from other inconveniences, was preparing to leave for Venice; but he was obliged to suspend his departure, for what happened three or four days after his hearing. I can tell it better than anyone; and I have to do it as much out of justice, as out of sensitivity for what these two senators suffered.

I played shuttle cocks, one afternoon, in the Baile's room with his son Joseph. We saw an aga enter with two Turkish slaves, who asked to speak to Baile Ciurani. We answered him through an interpreter who was at the city hall, that the Baile was resting. "I want to speak to him on behalf of the Grand Vizier," replied the Turk haughtily. The son continued that he was sleeping; and I urged him to go and wake him up. Finally, seeing that he did not want to do it, I left the game, and I went to warn the Baile of the arrival of the aga. This worthy senator answered me, "there is undoubtedly some new business on the carpet." He got dressed at the same time, and went to the audience room. An interpreter was called, and by chance a man named Peroni came, who reported on the request for the aga, conceived in these terms. "I am here on behalf of the Grand Vizier. All the Muslims of Constantinople have complained to him that you Venetians, under the faith of the treaties, came to take all the slaves with two warships. I want to visit them at this moment and take all that I find; and I want it done now." The Baile Ciurani, undisturbed, ordered pipes, coffee, sorbet, and jams; and having brought me to his chair, he whispered in my ear, "I have no one here. Please tell Procurator Morosini (who lived in another house not far away) what you heard; and added that I never knew that any slave had been hidden in the ships of the Republic, and that it would be my pleasure to have him instruct me how I should act on this occasion." I immediately went to Prosecutor Morosini. I found him sitting at a table, playing with a little dog he loved very much; and with the Doctor PIvati at his side. As soon as he knew the subject of my commission, he sent him away; and questioning me on all the circumstances of the speech of the aga, he put his hand on his forehead, and said to me these words thoughtfully. "I do not know that in our ships, we have ever removed any slave, but, as the Turks have assumed the right to visit ships at the castles of Dardanelles, it will be good, not to provide new pretexts

---

[32] Translator: A "*baile*" is a Venetian ambassador.

[33] Translator: The text says "chevalier", which is a "knight." "*Cavaliere*" is the Italian equivalent which seemed appropriate to insert.

for this animal of the Vizier, to promptly allow the visit requested by the aga. I salute, however, on my part, the Baile Ciurani, and tell him that after this visit, we will see each other this evening." I quickly returned to the Baile's house, to whom I communicated this answer. At the same time, he said to the Turk who ate jams, that he was welcome to make such search as he wanted on the ships, but that he would find no slaves there. At the same time, he ordered the interpreter to follow the aga, and to tell the officers on his part to let him visit the ships. The aga, on boarding, saw one of the slaves. This unhappy frightened man at the sight of the Turk fled; and hid among the ropes. The aga ran after him, through the soldiers of the Republic, to stab him. The soldiers, indignant at his behavior, threatened him, and he was forced to flee as quickly as possible, by the ship's ladder, and without *babouches*, and jump into the boat which had brought him. He made a report to the Vizier as one can imagine. So the next day there was a rumor spreading throughout Constantinople, that the Dragoman Tarsia had been called to the Kaiaja; that he had said to him in a proud and severe tone, that the Great Lord informed of what had happened about the Venetian ships, had resolved to secure the persons of the two bailes, and to have the Republic's ships taken to the Turkish shipyards, to disarm them, and dismantle them, in order to kill the large number of slaves who had to be hidden there. This narrow step was all the more easy to execute, after what had just happened, so that one saw on the channel the corpses of those who the sinking of some saiques (kinds of ships with only a sail, which the Turks use for the transport of goods) had perished in the Black Sea. (What happens often and even easily). Although one sees these corpses rotting by the sea and half eaten by the fish, the Turks used them as a specious pretext, to publish that they were the corpses of the slaves who had taken refuge in the ships of the Republic; and that the Venetians had perished miserably while hiding their crime. The ministers of the Christian powers, and the well-intentioned Turks, made all possible diligences, and the necessary steps, to bring the Vizier to abandon his claims; but everything was useless. The two senators resolved among themselves to re-embark on their vessels, and risking the vessels themselves, bearing the flag of the Republic. The Bash-Chiaous of the Porte came aboard the vessels, to make a visit, and he made it in the presence of the two senators, without finding any slave, but the Grand Vizier, was all the more obstinate. Finally, in such an embarrassment, everyone carried a different judgment. The two senators, by an intrepidity worthy of admiration, seemed resolved to sacrifice their lives in the Prisons of the Seven Towers, and to save the vessels to the mercy of chance, rather than it was said, that these two warships entered the port of Constantinople, under the faith of the treaties, on the occasion of a single slave having been introduced into one of these vessels, God knows by whom, which were disarmed in the arsenals of the Turks, that the bronze artillery was dismantled, and that the standard of the Republic was despised.

To return now to our subject, the captain of the largest vessel, called a "*bronza*," a native of Perastine, a man who had aged in the navy, and who had served during the Candia War, proposed to drive the ships out of the Dardanelles. He examined the nature of the current, the advantage of the night, the construction and the situation of the batteries of the castles, and moreover did what he considered the most expedient, but which it is not convenient for me to report here. This gave me an opportunity to learn what was going on in the navy, a passage which had always been regarded as impracticable, as I have said. Age and experience then taught me more, that the way in which this old captain surely passed through the straits was favored by the simple current, even in calm times.

I must say, to resume the thread of my story that the Grand Vizier seeing the unshakable firmness of the two senators and reflecting that the breaking of the Peace of Candia would have been inevitable, if he had persisted in wanting to take the ships in the shipyards, began to deal for a sum of money. The senators consented; but as modestly as possible, to avoid drawing their homeland into an expensive war. All being granted, the Procurator Morosini set sail for Venice, while the couriers carried to the Senate the news of the violence of the Grand Vizier, and how it had been appeased. This news was not well-received; and the senators, perhaps believing that it would have been better, according to their particular motives, to let the Turks act, recalled Senator Ciurani, and ordered that the sums paid as much by one as by the other, be reimbursed to the public, from their own income. It was necessary that the Republic had particular views, to have thus treated two worthy citizens, besides innocent on the origin of the evil, as I tried to report it, since Heaven provided me with the opportunity to know, as I have said, and to admire the valor and the fearlessness which they made appear, to preserve the honor of their fatherland at the risk of their lives. I admit the truth, the memory of these two worthy senators of such rare courage, will always be dear to me, in addition to the recognition that I must preserve for them; to Procurator Morosini, for the friendship with which he honored me; and towards Senator Ciurani, for the service he rendered me, when I was a slave of the Turks in Dalmatia. I sent him the letters I wrote to my family asking for my ransom, and he immediately sent a boat with a man laden with more money than was necessary; and to whom he ordered to buy me back at whatever cost. If he had not acted on this occasion as a true friend, I would not have been able to obtain my freedom, because the Republic having declared war on the Porte at that time, it would have been impossible for me to obtain the money for my ransom.

Now let's move on to the second description I promised. It is the custom of the Turks on St. George's Day, which is one of the last days of April, that their entire fleet (each a freshly tarred ship, painted in various colors, and decorated with flames), pass by the Seraglio. From there it reaches the shoals of the Sea of Marmara, to set sail, from where it comes to cross the Straits of the Dardanelles, to run through all the isles and roadsteads which belong to the Empire, and demand, at the same time, the tributes that the people owe, as well to the Public Treasury, as to the particular trading post of Capitan Pasha, or Commander of the Sea. This was practiced in 1680 in the same season; but with extraordinary splendor, which the reigning Sultan ordered it for his pleasure. Father Etienne, a French Capuchin, of exemplary virtue, made it possible for me to see this fleet comfortably. He was a very clever surgeon, and treated Capitan Pasha, who had a lot of regard for him. This general always led him in campaigns on his ship, which was a great relief for the poor Christian slaves of the islands and the galleys, because this good monk took advantage of the benevolence of the Turks, to be their intercessor on these occasions. I happened twice to go to Constantinople with this Capuchin dressed in his religious habit, and to meet the *General de la Mer* (admiral)[34] on horseback, in a great procession, who stopped, on seeing him, and conversed with him very colloquially.

The day the fleet left, this monk took me aboard the *Batarde*, the largest of the galleys, and boarded by Capitan Pasha. This ship had sumptuous crews, and I was within range of seeing all those mentioned in the *Canon-Name*, and of noticing the order of their march. Capitan Pasha had his galley approached and bridged a little over a *Ciosco*, or Sultan's Pleasure House. This house was outside Constantinople, and the Sultan, seated on his throne, received the homage of the general and all the other captains, who wore gold brocade garments, filled with Zubelines. The Grand Vizier was present at this ceremony, and he was standing with folded hands. As soon as all the officers, dressed in the same way, had passed according to the order established by the regulations of the navy, the first chiefs followed Capitan Pasha, who, a cane in his hand that was tall as a man and garnished with an ivory apple, walked at the head of all the officers, who paid court to the Grand Vizier. This one followed them to the *Batarde*, whose stern was all furnished with very rich cushions, on which they sat down, after the galley, having been saluted by its artillery, had passed the Sultan's *Ciosco*.

---

[34] Translator: At this time the French talked of the "naval army" instead of a "fleet" and referred to fleet commanders as "generals" instead of "admirals. This makes some parts of this translation very difficult, because it is occasionally unclear if they are talking about a general or an admiral.

The general showed the Grand Vizier the ships one after the other, and having passed the tip of the Seraglio, in the middle of the salvos of the Turkish fleet, and also of all the ships that were in the port, including the Christians, we prepared a splendid dinner. It consisted of a large quantity of meat, which was served almost as soon as it appeared, and a few people ate a lot. As soon as all these ships were offshore in the Sea of Marmara, they ranged in two wings, leaving in the middle the *Batarde* of Capitan Pasha. In this arrangement, I could notice the little experience that the Turks have in handling oars, especially with regard to the galleys that the *Canon-Name* calls a "zaccale." In these 15 oars were in the air, while ten remained in the water, which surprised me a lot in light of the beautiful order with which the Venetian galleys sailed, on which I had sailed to Corfu. Those called "*beglers*" sailed with less disorder, but there is no comparison with those of the Republic. Their galley slaves were poor Christian slaves, because the Turks will not do this, either willingly or by force. I examined the figure and the proportion of the ships, and I found them entirely similar to those of the Venetians, with the proviso that the sterns and the bows were higher. The Turks say that these ships were made in the shape of cucumber, and that they were given this height, so that they could better resist the storms so common in the Black Sea.

As soon as the fleet landed on the Isles, we saw a large number of very agile galiotes appear, among which there was one larger than the others, covered with gold cloth, on which the Grand Vizier, Capitan Pasha and four others from the first Chiefs of the Sea, went to Constantinople, and we followed them closely in another ship, the Capuchin and me. This fleet in this state, neither in the eyes of the militia, nor in relation to the Chiourmes, nor for the quality of the ships, could not have stood up to that of the Venetians. It is true that the six *maone*s were missing, which are in all things in conformity with the Venetian galleasses; and that were left in the shipyard, not being well-refitted; but when they would have been with the rest of the fleet, with such a *Chiourme*, they would have only increased the pomp of this sortie, by the diversity of the colors, the flames, the discharges of artillery and the cries of the *Chiourmes*.

Finally, I will report what I saw in the month of March, 1692. I very often went in that time in a boat to the Turkish shipyards, to assure myself more and more of what would seem incredible, that Christians of all nations directed the construction of the warships in the service of the Porte, and they caused the Turks to see the differences in the ships which they manufactured themselves, from what they constructed, which could not move, so that they would profit best from their instructions. The Grand Vizier Kiuperly was the author of this new shipyard, by the council of a Livornese Renegade, called Mahomet Aga. This man had entered the good graces of the Vizier, by proposing to him to issue a new, debased coinage[35], to compensate for the exhaustion of the Treasury, resulting from the extinction of the trade in all the Empire; whereupon the Vizier gave him the direction of the Office of Constantinople. In this close confidence, he proposed building warships with all the required proportions. He made a model of it which was then offered to me for sale; and he insisted that the Venetian fleet was superior to that of the Turks, by the great number of their warships. He said that the Porte lacked neither materials for building ships, nor artillery, nor ammunition with which to match them, and that he was responsible for bringing in these master workers, whom I then saw working, although the Vizier had died at the battle of Slankamen.

We know enough what the success of this renegade was; and we saw the fleet of Turks reinforced by well-proportioned warships, and mounted with large bronze guns, leave the Straits of the Dardanelles, and present themselves to that of the Venetians, which it had never dared to do, while it had only been made up of galleys. Whatever renegade was seen with a good eye at the Porte, the hatred of the people against him over the debased currency, which he founded, went so far that after the death of Vizier Kiuperly, he

---

[35] Translator: Debasing currency is the process of mixing base metal in with gold or silver so as to reduce the amount of precious metal in the coins, thereby creating more coins. This was a common practice in Europe when those rulers had financial problems and the populace could not be taxed any more.

was publicly beheaded at Adrianople, in the midst of the continuous howls of the Turks; and the Grand Vizier successor to Kiuperly, confiscated all his property, which consisted of a fairly large quantity of jewels. I myself took part in this picking over of his remains, gaining several Arab and Greek manuscripts. But what was the use of this Renegade's death if his work remained and will remain to the prejudice of Christianity? Notwithstanding all this, it will be able to prepare, as it should, to strike down the Turks at once, since the opportunity has not so far presented itself to test in a battle the maneuverability of these ships. They are, moreover, well-proportioned; wood was not spared, nor was artillery, and construction is easy, since, as we have seen in the *Canon-Name*, the Porte draws from its own states all that is necessary for the construction of his ships. In addition to that, experience and skill are required to maneuver these ships; and it does not appear how the Turks can gain it, except by the journey they make after their construction, from Constantinople to Corfu. I do not believe that the Turks can use their artillery with more dexterity at sea than on land, where I have noticed their little experience, both in their sieges and in their battles.

    Of all that remains, and what one can consider of the operations of the Navy, I already said in the beginning that I had very little knowledge of it, to speak of it, as I did military operations on land.

CHAPTER XXVII
The Turkish Fleet on the Danube.

So as to address everything that regards the Turkish naval forces, I wish to add to that which concerns their maritime armament that which concerns what they had on the Danube, and of which I have a greater knowledge.

In the past wars in Hungary, the Turks had on the Danube River a great number of ships with sails and oars, and well-armed. The stories mention it; and you can still see some in the Vienna shipyard, which were taken by the Imperials.

In 1689 this squadron, which was beaten around Vidin by the Imperials, was composed of three demi-galleys, six little brigantines, and a few other lesser ships. They were commanded by Ali Pasha, Captain Commander of the Danube. This fleet did not make much progress, because it found itself appalled at the defeat of the army.

Since in 1690 it appeared more numerous and better in order, I proposed that it was necessary to oppose its progress, by taking post on a small island near the Danube cataracts, which I had fortified, and which I called "*Carolina*," to honor the Archduke Charles, now Emperor. This advice had its effect; the Turks could not fail to attack it, but the accident which caused Belgrade to fall, resulted in it being abandoned, after it had long closed the Danube, during the same siege of Belgrade.

In 1691 the Turkish squadron appeared even stronger, having fortunately damaged our stores which were on boats; and it obliged the Imperials to have a squadron on this river, if not as abundant in oars, at least better supplied with artillery. In the following years, it was reinforced with more and more ships, which I distinguish belong of three kinds.

The first is the demi- galley and has 18 or 20 benches, with seats for two or three men on each. They had eight of these in 1694 when they came to form the siege of Peterwaradein.

The second, which is called, if I am not mistaken, a "*berghende*," had 14 to 16 oars, was lighter, and two men are enough for each bench.

The third consists of boats of 8 to 10 oars on each side, which need only as many men. There were in this way an infinite number of them when the above-mentioned siege was attempted; but, nevertheless, the multitude and the diversity of the banners they flew made their numbers appear much greater.

These ships are very light for movement, and very suitable for landing, because the sails and ropes are governed by good sailors. They descend with great speed, helped in this by the speed of the river, and they go back up, when the enemy allows it, with the help of people who pull them with ropes. The larger ships have two 6 to 8 pounder guns; and the others only 2½ pounders. During the siege of Belgrade, they were long drawn up in battle formation against me, who commanded on the bank of the Dniester, on the land side; and not being able to beat them with equality, I sent a detachment with cannon from the other side, to put them between two fires, but the Turks having taken off, and having approached our squadron from the front, because the situation of the fortress could not be extended, made such a heavy fire against the shore with their artillery, that the detachment was forced to withdraw, after a fairly considerable loss.

These kinds of ships, like the strongest fear shore batteries on the banks or on islands more than anything else. They beat them from all sides; and in narrow places, they have only the freedom to maneuver, which they can do much less, when having to suffer from enemy fire, while they still have to overcome the river's current.

The militia which is employed with this armament, has no regulations governing order, or numbers, which depends on the offensive or defensive operations. It is put ashore, or by disembarking conveniently, as it often happens, because the ships being already in the water, and the army on the banks of the river, we can take it in proportion as we need it, so it is sometimes more, and sometimes less numerous. It is certain that this militia is a confused mass of people who speak many languages, and who profess different religions, and even has a bunch of scoundrels. In the time I was in Constantinople, they came to spend the winter there, and they were recruited again in the spring. During this time, they made the highways unsafe, both for the Turks and for other nations, and the *Kaimekan* was forced to have the houses of the ambassadors guarded, to prevent any violation of the rights of the people in their regard.

There is at Rosgik, at the confluence of the Jantra River, which is the most considerable fortress on the Danube in Bulgaria, a shipyard that serves as a winter retreat for this squadron. I went there in 1691, when I was commissioned by the British Ambassador to compliment the above-mentioned Capitan Ali. This officer received me with great pomp, despite the noise of the workers who worked on the ship's refit. He showed me all that he was building himself, he praised to me especially 49 pontoons, as of his invention, designed to take cavalry and baggage across the river; but I only estimated number of people who were to ride these ships. This place is the ordinary residence of this officer; and besides that, the superintendency of Georg and all its dependencies in Wallachia.

CONCLUSION

The information that I have provided of the military state of the Ottoman Empire are founded primarily on the *Canon-Name*; then on the time I spent in Turkey at various times, where I profited from all the opportunities that the Turks afforded me, beginning with them and finally what I was able to gather of their military discipline when they made war.

It is now necessary to repeat here several things, the collection of which will give a brief knowledge of this state.

I have said that the first Turks, who founded the Ottoman Empire, came out of Tartary to seek suitable pasture for their herds. Driven by this motive, as useful as it was necessary, and finding Asia Minor torn apart by civil wars, having Morzar Erdegrul at their head, they became attached to a party. This joined them, and favored them, and by this means, Osman, son of Ercegrul, saw himself powerful enough to found this fatal empire.

To populate their small nation, which was to become mistress of so many others, the Turks thought of employing the Christians for this purpose, while making them embrace Islam.

Their number increased thereby; their militia consequently became more considerable, and they prevailed in a condition to make new conquests. They then settled the government of their nascent empire, which was made up of so many different Christian nations.

They formed a numerous people, who in their background were no longer either Turkish or Christian, but who were only a heap of all kinds of people delivered to superstition, lecherousness, greed and luxury, so natural among the Orientals. Prosperity made them proud and carried their empire to that point of extent and power where it was seen under Mahomet IV, whose decadence did not begin until the siege of Vienna was attempted.

The growth of this nascent Empire was in the beginning by divine permission; the Turks, however, behaved with great care, and the policies of so many nations which they associated, contributed little to it. They established laws, as much for their particular way of life, as for the governing of their Christian subjects, who were much more numerous than themselves. They knew how to use severity and gentleness at the right time, and violated their superstitious laws[36], by suffering that Christians established themselves in their Empire. This establishment was of great use to them, be it for the maintenance of the arts, or be it for trade. Finally, by a well-regulated economy, they made statutes, both for this last article, and for so many different kinds of militias, intended to serve on sea and on land.

These military statutes are in truth very remarkable but are not worthy of this impression that they made for so long, I do not say on the Christian subjects of the Turks, but on the most warlike Christian nations of Europe, who suffered cruel insults from the Turks, be it through fear or through a vile commercial interest, of which they should still be ashamed.

In the aftermath, many abuses have crept into these military regulations, which have caused great damage throughout the body of the Empire. The militia has run down, and soon it will be completely destroyed. Imperial authority is almost no longer recognized, and it will finally be completely lost.

Finally, I have shown, speaking of military operations, by the continual flight of the militia, what is its value, and what is the experience and the conduct of its leaders.

So, to follow the plan that I proposed in this collection, I come back to show in a shortcut, what are the revenues of the Ottoman Empire, and what is the number of militias maintained in its pay.

---

[36]Translator: By "superstitious laws" the author means the laws of Islam.

First we have to remember here this great expanse that the Empire had, from the mouths of the Nile, with the circuit that embraces part of Arabia and Persia, Georgia, the Maeotian Swamp[37], Muscovy, Podolia, and containing Transylvania and Hungary, to the Vag and the Rah, almost to the borders of Austria, and from there, embracing Illyria, Greece, the Azov Sea, the Black Sea, and the Capha Straits.[38] We must also remember that the nations which inhabit all these different countries are Christian, although infected with heresy, and that they speak different languages. We will then judge whether the Sultan's income, which constitutes the Porte's treasury, is sufficient for such a vast expanse of country.

---

[37] Translator: The swamps at the mouth of the Tanais River in Scythia.
[38] Translator: Probably the Kerch Straits.

STATE OF THE COMPANIES THAT FORMED THE TREASURY OF THE OTTOMAN EMPIRE IN 1683

The revenues of the Ottoman Empire are divided, as I have reported, in the first part of this military state, into several counting houses, that form the Treasury of the Porte. To have the total of all the sums reported in each counting house in particular, it is necessary to assemble them in this manner.

	Purses	Aspres
The Public Counting House of the Empire for Revenue ..	14,731	11,224
The subsidiary counting house or the counting house of the Sultan's stay in Andrianople	2,739½	
Principal Counting House of the Sultan, destined for his pleasures and which he can use as he pleases.	4,143½	10,000
The fourth, which is that of Mecca	821	70,074
The fifth which pays the Toprakli Militia and which is replenished with the product of the tithe, though the *Canon-Name* does not specify the sum, but it is reported to be about....................................	8,580	18,860
The sixth, which includes what we have said is paid in kind, has no evaluated price; and one cannot exactly determine the sum; however it is never less than…..	2,000	
The sum of the above……………………………..	32,416	70,178
I now want us to consider the profit which returns to the Treasury, by the benefit of time; that is to say by the difference of the solar year with the lunar, either by demanding, or by paying on the basis of this last year. It earns, every 33 years, about a year, and so every year a 33rd part of all the sums I have produced. It is thus necessary to take, of this total sum, the 33rd part, to join it then to the principal sum. This 33rd part will go up to …………………………………………	982	12,429
The two sums together come to …………………..	33,398	22,607
In addition, it is necessary to pay attention to the profit that the Treasury makes in the collection of the incomes, receiving the risdales on the basis of 80 *aspres* each, and making them pass on that of 120, and even of 140. One can calculate oneself this profit.		
I do not take into account the increase in types that a prince can make at all times and when, and on such a scale as he sees fit; the thing is too subject to variation.		

What we get from the main amount I mentioned, for the sole use of the militia, having many other sums to extract from it, to meet the costs which must be made, either for the pleasures of the Sultan, or for the care of Mecca, or for the maintenance of the Seraglio, and finally for all that has been mentioned above.

	Purses	Aspres	Soldiers
One has to pay the whole body of the Kapikulu Militia, which consists, as we have seen, of			74,148
Its maintenance requires................................	5,750		
One must also pay for the Toprakli Militia and the tributaries' troops, which come to.................			174,292
One must also pay for the Seratkuli Militia, or Frontier Militia, which we have designated above by the names of Asaps-Seimenis and Beslics and the like, which are increased in wartime, numbers are uncertain in peacetime; and consequently the sum that it is necessary for their maintenance, which one draws from the first or the second subsidiary counting house or from fines, it is certain that it is necessary to pay for a militia that comes to	13,287		248,440
This does not include the sum necessary for the maintenance of the Seratkuli Militia, nor the number of soldiers that form it for the reasons mentioned above.			

Examination of the Corps of This Militia, Which Forms That Which is Most Proper for War

	Purses	Aspres	Soldiers
The Janissaries are the best troops of the Kapikulu Militia. In 1680 they numbered.................			54,222
Of this number, one must deduct those who do not go into the field.			
One should also remove those who are destined to guard the frontiers of the Empire, which comes to			211,426
The *corigius* destined to guard the three Imperial residences, being in Constantinople, Adrianople, and Burse, which come to			430
The *uturacs*, which come to...........................			7,000
The *fodlacorans*, which come to			3,020
All these separate corps come to			34,876
One sees from this that the number of Janissaries, who go into the field is reduced to			19,346
We now go to the rest of the Kapikulu Militia:			
The *Agemoglans* come to			4,012
These do not go into the field.			

	Purses	Aspres	Soldiers
The number of *Topeys*, engineers, and *Sakkai* is indeterminate; it is sometimes larger or smaller; however, it leaves nothing that is remarkable.			
The *Gebegys* are in total …………………………			630
The third part are those that do not go into the field and their number is reduced to ……………...			420
Thus, the Kapikulu come, in total, to …………….			19,766
The Kapikulu Cavalry comes to ………………….			15,284
The third part of these corps do not go into the field, except with the Sultan and their normal number is………………………………………………			10,190
Thus, the Kapikulu Militia, both infantry and cavalry, which go into the field, come to ……………..			19,956

The Toprakli Militia

	Purses	Aspres	Soldiers
According to the tables, all this militia, including the tributary troops, as we have seen, come to …….			154,292
We must now observe in relation to this militia, the same division as for the Kapikulu, and distinguish that which is intended for the border guard, from those which marches on campaign. The latter is maintained by the provinces of the middle of the Empire; and at the first command of the Sultan, it forms with the Kapikulu and the tributary troops, the body of the offensive army, as I have shown in the preceding chapters. The other is entirely exempted from fighting, all the time, except for the part which is garrisoned in frontier fortresses, which is used to cover the army, which is to attack the enemy, and which is looked upon as a reinforcement. The rest of this militia, which is not employed in what I have just said, has nothing to do; however it does not stop increasing the body of the militia which marches on campaign; thus it is necessary to subtract from the Toprakli this part which remains inactive, in order to be able to judge to what rises an army made up of all the militias of the Sultan, as it was in 1683, which formed the siege of Vienna.			
These militias intended to march in the countryside, are provided by the following pashas:			

	Soldiers
Anatolia	17,826
Diarberir	2,597
Aleppo	2,152
SamSerif	3,606
Karas	367
Arzerun	11,577
Romelia	25,890
Bosnia	771
The tributary troops	28,000
The total of these troops comes to:	92,829
To see what can mount the largest army in the Ottoman Empire, we must also add to this part of the Toprakli Militia, which can be in the field, without losing that of the Kapikulu which we evaluated at	29,956
We also add to the army the body of frontier troops intended to cover the main army, the number of which, either Seratkuli or Toprakli, rises in the dependencies of Buda to	122,785
The Tartars, in addition, provide	10,000
These Tartars have a spare relay horse, and we see 40,000 horses, which are imposing at first, but which are hardly capable of supporting an important action. The 10,000 who are not paid as tribute are bought at a very great expense; and the Treasury spends it.	10,000
All these different corps of troops taken together form the most numerous army that the Porte can put into the field, nevertheless, according to the laws of which I have already spoken, they would all be forced to go; and this comes to …	142,785

These militias made up the Ottoman Army during the Vienna Campaign and following, until the Treaty of Karlowitz. Although this army was intended to make such an important siege, according to the above-mentioned calculations, the number of Janissaries from Constantinople was limited to 19,346. It is true that Cairo sent 2,000, but it was on condition that after having made two campaigns, they would be exchanged for such a number of those who were used in this city; thus I count them for compensation for these companies, which, as I have said, are intended for the pleasures of the Sultan, and serve him as hunting dogs, or for other uses, and so many others which fall sick during the marches or who exempt themselves by dint of money.	
It has always been believed that the Ottoman army in front of Vienna was 300,000 strong. We can agree; but in this number we must understand. This multitude of slaves that the Turks need for their luxury, and the large baggage trains that the pashas and the Toprakli Militia bring with them In addition to this, we must add this quantity of merchants from all the different tributary nations of which I have spoken, and this excessive number of workers of all kinds of professions, who turn the Turkish camp into trading city. Finally it is necessary to incorporate this mass of vagabonds who are attracted by the hope of the spoils that the Ottoman Army had first made, while passing the Raab. We can see by this that this increase in camp followers only served to consume the food and the fodder, and to make the flight more confused and more precipitate, for lack of courage, weapons, and a good military discipline.	17,826

The Ottoman Army 1683 to 1732

Division of the Ottoman Army in the Field

	Soldiers
In the first campaign against Vienna, the Ottoman Army had no other enemies to fight than the Imperials, also it was very numerous. But the King of Poland came to the relief of Vienna with all his forces. The Porte sent there all its forces with formed the number of troops listed above. However, it had no extraordinary naval force.	
During the following campaign, the Porte had two other enemies to fight, namely Poland and the Venetians. The Poles attacked Moldova during two campaigns.	
These two new enemies forced the Porte to divide its army into three corps. One of 25,000 Turks and 12,000 Tartars, commanded by a serasker, marched against Poland; and another of 25,000 went against the Venetians, which totaled…………………	61,000
In addition to this last corps of 25,000 men, intended against the Venetians, the Porte sent another 10,000 men who were taken from the corps of the Grand Army of Hungary, to reinforce the pashas who were on the coasts.	
Thus, of these three corps of the total of the army which was in Hungary against the Emperor there remained only …………	70,785
It must be reflected here that after the defeat at Vienna, the Turkish army was no longer so numerous, having regard to the fact that defeats usually occur on troops subject to mutiny.	
After the first two campaigns that the Poles no longer had such a considerable army, the Porte sent a serasker, with 15,000 Turks, to guard the bridge at Silistria over the Danube; and the Tartars only made a few campaigns in Hungary, even in very small numbers.	
The continual losses, which the Turks suffered in Hungary, diminished the number of their soldiers; so that in the campaign of 1686, during which the battle of Arsan took place, the Ottoman army totaled only. ………………………………	60,000
However, Grand Vizier Suleyman had been in Belgrade all winter to recruit soldiers for the militia himself, in order to form the most numerous army that the Porte had since the siege of Vienna	
In the following this same army consisted more than in 45,000 or…	
We must consider, as I said, that this army was made up of a lot of useless people; but you must have experienced it to judge it soundly.	50,000

Examination of the Losses the Turks have Suffered Since the Peace of Karlowitz and that of Passarowitz, By Which One Can See that Which Remains of Their General army, Speaking of the Time of Prosperity Of Their Empire and the Only of the Land Forces.

By the Peace of Karlowitz the Porte yielded to the Emperor all of Hungary, with the exception of the suburbs of Temeswar, all of Transylvania, all of Slavonia, with the exception of the small lower angle of Sarvisch, opposite Belgrade, all the part of Bosnia, which is on the borders of the chain of these mountains, on the side of the Sava and the One. It also ceded to Poland the city of Kamieniec and a small canton in the upper part of Moldova. The Czar received Azov and the new forts on the isles of the Dnieper; and the Venetians acquired all of the Morea[39] and a number of important places in Dalmatia. The Peace of Passarowitz was even more disadvantageous to the Sultan, because he ceded by this peace to His Imperial Majesty all the suburbs of Temisvar, that of Belgrade and all of Lower Serbia, located below the Danube. In addition, he also gave him part of the high mountains where Upper Serbia begins, towards the Timoc River, all that part of the Banal Wallachia, which ends at the Iron Gates of the Danube, as far as the confluence of the Luta and along this river to the ends of the Transylvanian Mountains.

On the side of Poland and Muscovy there was nothing new from this peace, these two powers having had no part in the war which preceded it. Besides this, the Czar in a war which he waged on his own, lost the forts of the Dnieper and Azov. The Venetians also lost the Morea; but on the other hand they pushed their conquests in Dalmatia and in Albania. As a balance to the present state of this empire one must understand the impact the losses of the fortresses, which are now in the power of the Christians, it is easy to judge that its decay comes mainly from the vast and important conquests that the Emperor made on his side.

We cannot calculate exactly how much money the Porte demanded from all of Hungary, from Transylvania, from Slavonia, from Lower Serbia and from that part of Wallachia, which was called Banale; but we may well list the parts from, which the first counting house of the Empire drew money. These parts are the saltworks, the customs, the tolls, the rights of fishing, and so many other small rights that this same counting house took in Constantinople, where, it was used largely for the payment of the Seratkuli Militia.

With regard to the counting house intended for the payment of the Toprakli Militia, to which the proceeds of the tithes are brought, it is easy to assess the loss of the lands mentioned above, by the number of ziamets and timars, and by the dependencies of the pashas and the belgas, although, as I have said, two circumstances which arose at the death of the owners of these districts, prevented their income from being properly calculated. We cannot also calculate exactly how much the loss of Transylvania, whose prince bore the title of king, amounted to because it was a tributary; and there is no certainty that the annual tribute in money. The sum which came from it was nothing, in comparison with what the prince, and the factions which were against him sent to the Porte at present, and especially to the ministers. They lost more there than the Treasury; and the same thing happened with respect to Wallachia. Thus, in examining this loss, what is most considerable is the militia, which must strengthen the Ottoman Army.

The conquests of the Venetians, especially in Dalmatia, joined to those of the Emperor on the same side, have so squeezed the Pasha of Bosnia, that there remains only one, small stretch towards the top of the mountains, by which it joins the frontiers of the Empire, on the mountains of Herzegovina and Albania.

Therefore, there remains to the Ottoman Empire only a part of the Pashala of Bosnia and Romelia, and it can only use it as a border, unable to camp there, to march, for example, against Persia. It only has

---
[39]Translator: Morea was the name of the Peloponnese peninsula in Southern Greece.

the freedom to reinforce there, its army in case it wants to try to recover its conquests in Europe.

The capture of Kamieniec closed the path for Tartar raids into Poland; but, on the other hand, the Porte was spared the expense that it was obliged to make for the maintenance of a large number of Janissaries garrisoned in this fortress. In this way, Moravia, tired and trampled by the marches and counter-steps of this garrison, found itself at rest, because the dependencies were entirely ruined, and the Turks did not profit from this fortress; reasons which facilitated the restitution, without which the League would never have consented to any preliminary peace. A few years later, the Turks violated the Peace of Karlowitz, by building forts on the Dniester; and constructed at Cucin vis-à-vis Kamieniec, a fortress which closed to the Poles the passage of the Varco in Moldavia, under a captious pretext, which was ordinary to the Turks, that it was to keep in respect the Tartars of the Budgiack, but under cover the dependencies of Bender, another fortress on the Dniester.

Spahi in 1696 by Manesson

We Pass Now to an Examination of the Precise Losses Mentioned Above

	Soldiers
The revenues that the first counting house drew from certain locations was lost, thus it is necessary to understand this loss from the maintenance of a very large number of militia soldiers. This was truly considerable, since by it the Porte found itself deprived of a powerful reinforcement of Albanian infantry, to sustain the Janissaries in case of need, as it occurred in the last wars. The loss of this infantry came from that part of Albania, which became the border of Lower Serbia.	
The Porte lost the maintenance of the Seratkuli Militia in the aforementioned kingdoms and provinces.	
The loss of Transylvania cost it …………………………………..	8,000
By the loss of part of Wallachia, it is necessary to subtract at least the militia from that province ……………………………………..	1,500
All of Moldavia, which furnished ……………………………………	4,000
It was entirely ravaged.	
The Porte also lost a part of the Pashala of Bosnia and this loss came to:	772
Part of that of Temisvar, which furnished ………………………..	667
And the part of Buda, which it was obliged to surrender …………….	1,269
All these losses come to …………………………………………..	16,108
Thus, all the militia which, during the prosperous period of the Empire, came to ……………………………………………………………..	248,440
Since it is necessary to subtract 16,108, it is reduced to …………	232,332

	Soldiers
We have seen that during this period, the Ottoman army destined to march into the field in case of war came to ………………………………..	142,785
Thus, it is necessary to see what the loss amounted to in order to judge what remained to be maintained.	
One must remove those resulting from the loss of Transylvania ………….	8,000
By the loss of part of Wallachia ………………………………………..	1,500
By the desolation of Moldavia ………………………………………….	4,000
Total losses …………………………………………………………….	13,500
The Pachalas of Romelia and Bosnia could provide nothing, either for the army in Europe or in Asia, for the above reasons alleged, however, wile they supplied …………………………………………………….	26,662
Thus, if one removes from the army, such as it was in the prosperous times, these two numbers of militia, which, taken together are ……………	40,162
	102,623
There does not remain presently for the total of the army than ……..	

The Division of This Army in the Same Manner As During the Times of Prosperity

	Soldiers
The Porte sent 25,000 Turks and 12,000 Tartars against Poland. They sent an equal number against the Venetians and 10,000 others to guard the coasts, as I have said, which comes to a total of ……………………..	72,000
This brings the total of the troops sent against the Emperor at …………….	30,623

The State of the Turkish Navy

	Sailors
The Turks, as I have said earlier, did not pass beyond the Straits of the Dardanelles, before the year 1691; and their naval forces consisted of sailing ships and galleys, as I have described, which could not face the Venetian fleet. This naval force, as I have spoken of in an earlier chapter, consisted of officers, workers, soldiers, *chiourme*, and militia from the Pashalas situated in the islands dependent to the Empire and came to……………………………………………………………………..	50,572
The Porte maintained the same number of light ships in the Turkish fleet and it was augmented by 30 warships. Thus, the number mentioned above had become insufficient; and it was consequently necessary to have more sailors, soldiers, bombardiers, and a *chiourme*, more numerous, which required an augmentation of 10,000 to 12,000 men	
From there, it is easy to judge that the Porte was obliged to make more expenditures than before, for these 30 warships, that as I already said, I saw being built in Constantinople; it is necessary to add to this the maintenance of these ships, what it costs to launch them and remove them to fit them with artillery, and all the necessary equipment. This expenditure thus increased the expenditures of that of the Treasury, since it costs much more for the maintenance of the whole fleet, than when it was composed only of light ships.	
The Porte cannot dispense with maintaining a fleet when it is at war with the Venetians; thus it made a great expenditure for ships, galleys, *chiourme*, workers, construction of ships; and in a word for all that is necessary for the Navy.	
So adding to the old Navy ………………..	50,572
An increase of at least ………………………………………………	10,000
Today it has ……………………………………………………	60,572

To See What Forms all the Military Forces of the Turks, In Always Observing the Same Comparison in the Time Of Prosperity of the Empire with its Present State Adding the Troops of the Navy to Those of the Army

	Soldiers
The troops from the time of peace came to	248,440
To this we add the state of the Navy	50,572
As a result, all the forces of the Navy and the Army come to	299,012
We have seen that at the same time the Army only had in the field	142,785
Thus, in adding the Navy, all the forces of the Empire consisted of	193,357
Dividing the total of these troops into three corps, on one side of 25,000 Turks and 12,000 Tartars facing the Poles, as I have already said, this gives	37,000
Then adding the 25,000 men facing the Venetians and the 10,000 coast guards. Adding to these all in the navy comes to	50.572
The army facing Poland and the Venetians comes to	122,572
There remains facing the Holy Roman Emperor	70,783

Solak of the Guard, 1574 (Bremen University)

Union of the Present States of the Navy And the Army

	Soldiers
We have already remarked that the army's militia today totals	232,332
This number added to the Navy comes to ………………………………	60,572
This gives a total of …………………………………………………….	292.904
We have already noted that the Army that enters the field today consists of ..	102,623
One must take from this state of the Navy the Pashalas of Cassa and Trebisonde which furnished ……………………………………	1,117
Thus, the total of the Navy and Army of the Ottoman Empire comes to …	162,078
Dividing the army that is in the field, containing, as I have said………….	72,000
Between the Polish and the Venetians, adding to these latter the Navy of ..	59,445
This gives a total of ……………………………………………………..	131,455
There remains an army corps of ………………………………………….	30,623
To act against the Holy Roman Emperor.	
But, if the war was in Hungary, as it has been earlier, the two Pashalals of Romelia and Bosnia could furnish to the army 15,000 to 20,000 men ..	20,000
The remainder shall serve, as said before, to guard the coasts.	
Thus the Army of Hungary against the Holy Roman Emperor would consist of …………………………………………………………………….	50,623
What would happen if the Porte has a fourth enemy on their hands, such as the Czar in the time of the Quadruple Alliance? This monarch has reduced the Tartars to not knowing or giving their head to find many men, and they will not have any effect other than defending against him, due to the sterility of the Ukraine and the lack of a fleet in the Maeotian Swamp.[40]	

Remarks Which Prove the Little Regard Which One Should Make of the Turkish Army

These troops which appear by the enumeration, so considerable on paper, will be found in the bottom very little things, if one examines how far their weakness goes, be it in relation to the quality of the soldiers, or in with regard to their armaments and their discipline. The Porte, considering the vast expanse of the Empire, is obliged to employ them not only against enemies from without, but also for the safety of the highways: Besides, dispersed as they are, what penalties would they suffer by bringing them together, with the exception of the Kapikulu Militia, which is still in Constantinople? In addition to that, there are so many falsely mustered men among the Toprakli Militia! The Turks themselves admit that one sixth of the rolls of this militia can be eliminated, and that it is impossible for half of it to enter the field when a war lasts more than three years. Five thousand *aspre* are not enough to support a soldier; and the zaims and the timariots must make up for what they skim in times of peace. When the war is longer than peace has lasted, and three years has passed, the Porte begins to turn a blind eye to these kinds of abuses. It is committed to it by the impossibility where the zaims and the timariots are then to lead to the army the number of troops,

---
[40] Translator: The swamps at the mouth of the Tanais River in Scythia.

which they must provide, especially those which are far from the theater of war, as for example, to come from Arzerun in Hungary. The savings which they make consists in carrying provisions to their troops or with carts or on horses, because, when these supplies are running out, they find themselves in the need to buy them at great expense from the vivandiers.

Besides that, the Toprakli and Seratkuli Militias are nothing other than what we call provincial militias; but much worse, since they do no service; and are not disciplined, like ours, languishing in the depths of the provinces of the Empire in idleness. They must not be taken into account. Thus, all the forces of the Ottoman Army are reduced to the Kapikulu Militia.

Objections That Can Be Made to These Remarks
And a Response to Those Objections

One cannot object, by chance, to this which I have said, that the Porte easily recruits its troops, as one has seen since the siege of Vienna to the Peace of Karlowitz, and though the Turks were frequently beaten, they were not long in returning to the field.

To this I respond that the Turks take flight at the right time, abandoning their tents, cannon, and baggage, and that they then rally a short distance from the battlefield, having new tents and other artillery already ready for them. However, they could profit from this advantage in the battle of Lenta, where their infantry found itself locked between the Teisse and the enemy's fire, the bridge being broken, so they were entirely destroyed as in the assaults on Naisel, Buda, and Belgrade. If they had three consecutive defeats, like those of Lenta, they should have made peace, being unable to replace their infantry. There is a proverb among the Janissaries, "Have a good eye and good legs;" to observe the inconsistence of the cavalry, which was prone to flight and the good legs were needed to follow them.

It will be objected, could they not make a general armament, or, without comparison a crusade?

I answer, as I have already done, that after the loss of Nasa and Vidin, this expedient was proposed in the Divan, but it was rejected.

It will also be asked, can the Porte not increase the revenue of the Treasury by new taxes on the subjects of the Empire, since the Turks do not want to suffer?

I reply that this proposal was rejected for the reasons that everyone can easily imagine. We asked in the Divan of the Mufti, if they could place a surcharge on the *Vacup* incomes, which are without comparison, like our ecclesiastical incomes, for the maintenance of mosques, hospitals, highways, bridges, schools, and hostels which absorbs millions of risdales every year, he replied that he would not: and alleged the reasons for this impossibility.

Could we not, it will be asked, have recourse to the Counting House Confiscations, to have enough to do with new levees?

The amounts that enter this counting house are uncertain, I will answer; and are for the benefit of the Vizier and the other ministers who control the administration.

This counting house, during the splendor of the Empire, under the reign of Sultan Mahomet IV, was filled with an infinity of confiscations, and in particular that of the Grand Vizier Kara Mustapha, which must have been very considerable. With all this, in 1687, when this Sultan was deposed, and the Public Treasury was exhausted, this counting house could provide very little for the maintenance of the militia. In order to provide for it, it was necessary to melt a quantity of silver harness from the horses of His Highness, to strip his slaves of their jewels, and to send back his concubines. However, the Treasury did not take advantage of everything put together, 1,500 purses.

In truth this sum is very small; those who had deposed Muhammad, however, exaggerated it, in order to show that this prince had been justly stripped of the Imperial dignity, as a prodigal, since of this large number of purses that had been received by the Confiscation Counting House, they found so little. This deposition was made with so little order, that the women who were expelled from the Seraglio could not be prevented from looting a quantity of furniture, and especially jewelry, which they sold at very low prices to the Christian merchants who were in Constantinople, who were making a good profit from these. Besides the little funds that must be made on these confiscations, we must also consider that the Turks, as I said above, have a habit of hiding their money and their jewelry in the ground. We attributed this custom to the little money that was found in Kara Mustapha Pasha's palace, and when he was strangled with such haste, his killers failed to make him confess where he had hidden his riches.

Dellis 1570's by Knotel (*NYPL*)

During the last wars in Morea[41] and at Belgrade,[42] the Grand Vizier, who had aroused them, used the way of confiscation, to seize the great wealth, be it money, or be it in jewelry, of the Prince of Wallachia, so as not to worry the Sultan, a stingy man, if ever there was one. During those of Hungary, these same means were used, when the occasion was found.

Here is this empire, which was invincible for two centuries, and the terror of Christianity, which in 1683, in the highest period of its prosperity, could only set up an army as I have described it. Its victories were confined to the capture of Belgrade, even if only by chance; and at the battle where General Veterani, having only 6,000 men, was attacked by the Sultan, at the head of the entire Ottoman army, at which time the Emperor was obliged to make such a great diversion in the Empire, while His Highness was supported by the Albanians.

If anyone objected to what I just said that the Turks had reconquered all of Morea in one campaign, I would answer that they made this conquest by violating the Peace of Karlowitz. Declaring war on the Venetians, and entering into the field, was the same thing with them, so all their forces, on land and at sea, attacked at the same time a power too weak to resist them on that side. On the other hand, when the Imperial army, reinforced by the Venetians, entered Hungary, the Turks were not only beaten as usual; but they also lost the two important fortresses of Belgrade and Temesvar, from where they were driven out; and were forced to ask for peace. If they had not been granted it, although neither Poland nor the Czar had joined the war, and the Venetians had withdrawn, the Christians would have seen the sad state to which the Ottoman Empire would have been reduced in Europe. Hard currency was rare

---

[41] Translator: Peninsula of Southern Greece.
[42] The Belgrade campaign has crowned Prince Eugene of Savoy with glory, the army of the Emperor having never won more complete or more striking victories.

there were no longer good militia, nor experienced captains; and the Turks feared a revolt of their own Christian subjects, among whom, oppressed as they are, there is no lack of people of spirit, attentive, not only to take advantage of the proper moment to shake off the Ottoman yoke, but also to set themselves up as sovereigns of their nations.

The feeling of the Turks about their emperors is that all the successors of Suleyman the Great were either tyrants or effeminate; and that is why they submitted the sultans to the power of the militias, among which it is impossible for there to arise any rebellions which would finally cause the ruin of the Empire. This ruin will happen, and even soon, above all, if not only the neighboring powers pay attention to their true interests, to what they should, to the support of religion and to the safety of their subjects; and if those who are far away do what they promised God on ascending their thrones. To entirely overthrow the Ottoman power, they have only to make a treaty between them which, stifling this fatal jealousy which divides them, fixes this balance if desired. This jealousy makes them leave in peace an empire that is the enemy of God and prevents them from pushing back the impious Muslim Sect to the ends of Arabia, where it was born, and from delivering this part of Europe and Asia, which is made up the old Greek Empire.

They only have to march, and without fighting, each has only to put themselves in possession of what will have fallen to it in sharing by the treaty of alliance, awaiting the little resistance that the Turkish militia can make, as I have described it, and the state of the finances of the Ottoman Empire. It may happen that I made an error of 25,000 to 30,000 men, and 2,000,000 or 3,000,000 *risdales* of annuities in the calculations I have given; however what I have said is sufficient to demonstrate to the princes and the people that the forces of the Turks have been nothing and are nothing in depth, and will in the future be only a pure punishment of Divine Justice against us, who use such a weak empire to punish us for our faults.

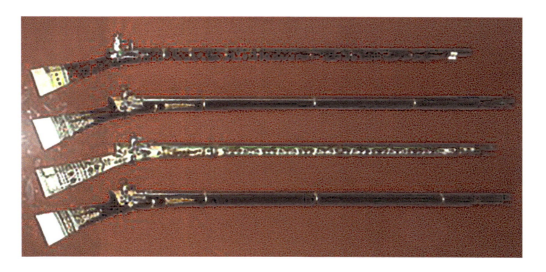

Turkish Muskets, (*Army Museum Paris*)

The Ottoman Army 1683 to 1732

A NOTE ON UNIFORMS[43]

The Ottoman Army was composed of people from Africa to Asia, so while there was a certain amount of uniformity, there was also a great deal of local variations. The main armies of the Porte migth have a sense of uniformity, but the troops of provincial governors or irregulars wuold contain a local "flair".

According to King, the headgear for foot troops consisted of a low, round, flat-topped hat wrapped in a cloth *Keffiyeh*. Mounted troops had a taller hat that flaired out slightly at the top.

Muskets varied during the period from matchlock, arquebuses and flintlocks. Pistols were also carrid by some officers and cavalrymen, from wheelocks to flintlocks.

(Left) Ottomna Yataga, which was a long sword or sabre which was used for infantrymen. (Wikipedia)

(Right) Ottoman Kilij was a sabre used by mounted troops. (Wikipedia)

Janissary in full dress, 1700 (NYPL)

CAVALRY

The "lance" carried by Ottoman cavalry was typically nie to ten feet long. They often carried a bow in a waterproof case as well as a quiver slung over his back. The saddle was often covered with a small square red blanket often with a contrasting border. Cavalry often carried small metal shields to protect the rein hand from attacks.

---

[43] Information comes from *Renaissance Armies 1480-1650* by George Gush, (Patrick Stephens: Cambridge, 1975), *Uniforms of the World* by Richard Knotel, Herbert Knotel and Herbert Sieg (Charles Scribner's Sons: New York, 1980) and *The Janissaries* by David Nicolle (Osprey Publishing: London, 1995).; *Great Northern War Compendium*, Vol II edited by Stephen L. King, Jr (THGC Publishing: St Louis, 2015)

Sipahi

Sipahi were divided into two groups – The Sipahi of the Porte were paid regulars, while the other was feudal cavalry. The latter reported for duty with the equipment necessary but were not uniformed in any fashion.

Sipahi's of the Porte had Light lances were painted green. Sipahi of the Porte wore highly decorated jackets and kaftans in scarlet, violet, dark blue and green with gold or silver embroidery. The boots were often yellow. The turbans were always white with red or purple caps and black feathers. Some units wore armor, but by the early 18th century all carried lances, firearms and swords.

Light Cavalry

For light cavalry green or blue caftans were worn as well as white, yellow violet and light brown.

According to Knotel, the Dellis wore panther skins and eagles feathers in their caps and wings on their shields.

Tartars often wore long coats, shirt, trousers and short yellow boots. Coats were often green or blue. They wore low round or conical red hats trimmed with brown fur.

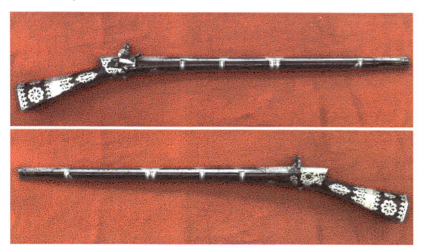

(Left) Ottoman miquelet, at type of flintlock from the late 17th/early 18th century (Wikipedia)

(Right) Ottoman cannon from end of 16th century (Wikipedia)
(Above) Ottoman artilleryman late 17th century from Ralamb Costume book

INFANTRY

The Janissaries started out as armored warrios equipped with a sword, spear and bow. As time went on, they dropped the armor, spear and bow in favor of the musket.

The Janissaries were typically clad in uniform colors by *Orta*. Tunics were often blue, red, green, purple and black. The trousers were often blue with yellow stockings. The "sleeve-cap" (often called the *zarcola* or *bork*) was white felt with a band of silver and gilt. The front of the hats traditionally had a plume holder to holed a feather given as a reward. Officers would have plumes of bird feathers. The boots were red for enlisted men and yellow for officers.

There were small units of armored infantry known as *ztrhli nefer*.

The Expedition to Revan under Murad III

Siege of Szigetvar, 1566

Specific musket bearing ortas were known as *sekbans*. They often dressed in blue or red, blue or green jackets. After the 1600's they became the dominant type of Janissary troops.

Solak's were archers. In the 1580's the Solak of the Guard were dressed in white, with a gold helmet and sash. Other uniforms consisted of a white or red turban with a gold band. The kaftans were red or yellow with red, yellow or green jackets and white feathers.

Turkish Azap Infantrymen often had white turbans, green caps, white and green striped shirts. The coat was red or green and the pants were green or blue.

Non-Turkish troops such as Bosnians and Balkan troops often had red caps with jackets of red, blue or brown. They had white leggings, black shoes and red leather equipment.

ARTILLERY

Ottoman artillerymen were often uniformed in yellow with green trim, red and yellow or green and black. Thier headgear was often a tall round hat made of red felt with black fur or a yellow turban or black round fur hat.

MINERS AND SAPPERS

Miners and sappers wore long kaftans in red, yellow blue or green. The had tall red fez's with either fur bands or white turbans.

STANDARDS

The various regiments of the Sipahi had different flags to denote them. The Kapikulu had red flags, the Silhidars had yellow, the Olufeci units had red and white and green and white. The feudal Sipahi's had standards according to the taste of the local governors. For horsetail standards were often white decorated with red and blue ribbons using red poles.

Sekbah ortas often carried red and sometimes striped flags.

The infantry and cavalry flags were often made with square, pointed tails or swallow tailed ends. Each units had its own color combinations. Typical combinations often included yellow, red and yellow stripes or yellow, white and yellow.

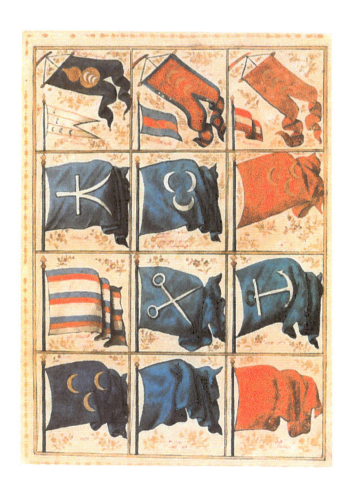

Naval Flags of the Ottoman Empire

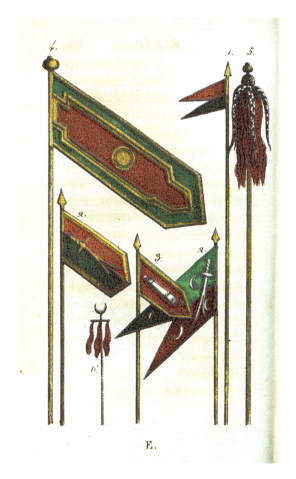

Cavalry Banner

Index

A
Adrianople, 85–86, 103, 131, 137
Advanced guard, 62, 74, 93
aga, 9, 15, 52, 55, 88, 91, 95, 128
age, 30–31, 97, 127, 129
Albania, 11, 30, 104, 142–43
Albanian Infantry, 77, 103, 143
Albanians, 77, 82, 103, 149
Aleppo, 85, 139
Anatolia, 30, 50, 52, 61–62, 66, 85, 94, 113, 139
Arabia, 31–32, 135, 149
Arabs, 10, 31, 131
Arat Pasha, 77, 101
Armenians, 54, 117
arms, 9–10, 13, 16, 19, 22, 30, 77, 91, 103, 108
army, main, 36, 139, 151
arquebuses, 91, 151
arquebusiers, 89
Arsan, 52, 57–58, 71, 75, 141
artillery, 22, 57–58, 61–63, 68, 71, 73–75, 91–94, 99–101, 103–5, 118, 120, 130–32, 145, 148
artillery and baggage, 73, 75, 93, 100
Artillery Corps, 53
artillery pieces, 24, 70
asna-agag, 28–29
Austria, 26, 33, 101, 108, 135
Azaps, 117
Azov, 142

B
Baden, 65, 77–78, 80, 94, 101, 104
baggage carts, 63, 74, 91, 104
baggage wagons, 50, 74, 82, 95
batteries, 75, 80, 82, 100, 103–4, 108, 110–11, 113, 115, 122–23, 129
battle, order of, 59, 70–71, 77, 96–97, 99–100, 103
battle formation, 57, 73, 80, 96, 100, 104–5, 132
battle of Arsan, 57–58, 141
battle of Slankamen, 9, 36, 42, 80, 104, 131
battle of Zenta, 94, 104
Bavaria, 100–101, 120
Belgrade, 25–26, 85–86, 91, 94, 100–101, 103, 106, 113, 117–18, 122–23, 125, 132, 141–42, 148–49
besiegers, 93, 99–100, 115, 118, 122
Black Sea, 30, 106, 113, 129–30, 135
Bosnia, 11, 30, 84–85, 94, 139, 142–44, 147
Buda, 21–23, 93, 96–97, 99, 115, 117–18, 120, 122–23, 125, 139, 143, 148
   first siege of, 115, 118
   lower city of, 120
   second siege of, 26, 118

Bulgaria, 50, 96, 133
Bulgarians, 74, 108, 116
Burse, 8, 127, 137

C
Cairo, 19, 31, 91, 140
caissons, 116, 120, 122–23
campaign plan, 58
camp in front of Vienna, 41, 59
Candia, 19, 22, 106–8, 110–13, 115, 117, 125, 129
Candia and Vienna attacks, 110
cannon, 19, 21–24, 36, 38, 70–71, 73, 75, 93–94, 96, 100, 104, 107, 115–16, 118
Canon-Name, 7, 13, 127, 130–31, 134, 136
Capitan Pasha, 130–31
carriages, 22–23, 30, 52, 84
cavalry, 12, 17, 19, 30, 50, 57–58, 70–71, 73–75, 77–78, 80, 84–85, 91–97, 99–101, 103–4, 151
   feudal, 58, 151
Chiaous-Pasha, 94–95
company, 8–9, 42, 45, 54, 89, 91–92, 108, 111, 136, 140
Company of Janissaries, 45
Constantinople, 8–9, 28, 30–31, 52, 57, 59, 85, 113, 127–31, 133, 140, 142, 145, 147, 149
counting house, 136, 142, 148

Crete, 19, 22, 28, 106–8

D
Dalmatia, 129, 142
Danube, 30, 70–71, 78, 80, 82, 86, 93–94, 99–100, 104, 111, 115, 132–33, 141–42
Dardanelles, 113, 115, 127–31, 145
Dnieper, 106, 113, 115, 142
Dniester, 106, 132, 143
Drava, 70–71, 99–100
drummers, 74, 88–89
drums, 39–40, 88–89, 92
Duke Charles, 75, 100

E
Egypt, 85
Egyptian Janissaries, 19
entrenchments, 57, 59, 70–71, 73–75, 77–78, 80–82, 84, 97, 100, 103–4, 111, 122–23, 125
Eugene, Prince, 84, 94

F
fascines, 33, 108, 110, 116
firearms, 11, 13, 16, 19, 21, 107, 152
flags, 36–38, 91–92, 117, 129, 154
fleet, 127, 130–32, 145, 147

flight, 73, 78, 93, 96, 99–100, 105, 125, 140, 148
fortifications, 113, 115, 117–18, 123, 125
   defensive, 125
fortresses, 21–22, 25–27, 56–58, 101, 104, 106–8, 110–13, 115, 117–18, 120, 122–23, 125, 142–43
frontier militia, 117, 137

G

Gallipoli, 85
General Aisler, 104–5
General Veterani, 23, 65, 93, 100, 104–5, 149
Germans, 71, 78, 100, 104, 113, 123
Grand Vizier, 36, 41, 44, 57–59, 61–62, 68, 70–71, 73–74, 84–85, 91–92, 95–97, 99–100, 128–31
Grand Vizier Kara Mustafa, 65, 108
Grand Vizier Kara Mustafa Pasha, 128
Grand Vizier Kara Mustapha, 148
Grand Vizier Kara Mustapha Pasha, 66, 68
Grand Vizier Köprülü, 9, 42
Grand Vizier Pery Pasha, 127
Grand Vizier Soleiman, 92
Grand Vizier Suleiman-Pasha, 23
Grand Vizier Suleyman, 141
Grand Vizier Suleyman Pasha, 57–58, 73
Greece, 30, 50, 104, 135
Greeks, 54, 96, 108, 113, 117

H

Heavy Matchlock, 19–20
Heraklion, 19, 22, 28, 106–8
Holy Roman Emperor, 146–47
horse tails, 38, 58, 88–89
horse tails and standards, 89
Hungary, 26, 30, 57, 73–74, 85, 92, 106, 115, 117, 132, 135, 141–42, 147–49

I

Imperial army, 41, 57, 70–71, 73, 77–78, 80–82, 84, 93–94, 97, 99–101, 103–5
Imperialists, 94, 103, 105, 118
infantry, 11, 57–58, 70–71, 73–74, 77–78, 80, 82, 84–85, 91–92, 95–97, 100–101, 103–4, 106, 148, 152

J

Janissaries, 8–11, 17–19, 44–45, 54–55, 58–59, 61–63, 73–75, 80, 91–92, 94–97, 99, 101, 103–4, 108–12, 117, 137, 143, 151–52
   new, 9–10
Janissary company, 42, 44
Janissary Corps, 9, 91
Janissary tent, 44
Jeghen Pasha Dondar, 61, 66, 95, 101

K

Kamieniec, 106, 142–43
Kapikulu, 11–12, 92, 138–39, 154
Kapikulu Cavalry, 15, 36, 38, 52, 58, 61, 63, 68, 138
Kapikulu Militia, 9, 137–38, 147–48
Kapikulu Sipahi, 36, 52
Kara Mahomet Pasha, 108
Kara-Mustafa, 50
Kara Mustapha Pasha, 149
Karlowitz, 42, 84, 105, 113, 125, 140, 142–43, 148–49
King John Sobieski, 96
Köprülü, 9
Köprülü, Achmet Pasha, 80
Köprülüzade Numan Pasha, 52

L

latrines, 41, 44, 65
Lorraine, 70–71, 73, 75, 97, 99–100, 118, 120, 122
Louis, Prince, 65, 77–78, 80, 94, 101, 103–4
Lower Serbia, 142–43
Luigi Marsigli, 5–155

M

Mahomet IV, 41, 134
   invincible Emperor Sultan, 94
Marmara, 85, 127, 130
Marsigli, Count Luigi Ferdinando, 5, 82
Mecca, 50, 136
militia, 5, 7, 9, 17, 19, 62–63, 85, 89, 91, 96–97, 105, 108, 131–38, 140–45, 147–49
Mohacs, 57, 73, 96, 100, 105
Moldavia, 30, 86, 143–44
Moldavians, 62, 65, 74, 93–94
Morava River, 93–94, 101, 103
Morea, 142, 149
Muhammad IV, 52
Murad III, 154
muskets
   flint-lock, 20
   long, 11
Mustafa, Kara, 73, 85, 91

N

Naisel, 113, 117–18, 120, 125, 148
navy, 127, 129–31, 145–47
Nişanci Suleyman Pasha, 57
Nissa, 75, 77, 85, 101, 103, 113
   battle of, 9, 77
   besieged, 106
Nissa River, 77
Non-Turkish troops, 153

O

oda, 8–9, 42, 45, 54, 89, 91, 94, 108

Oseck, 68, 70–71, 73, 75, 84, 94
Oseck Marsh, 57, 71, 73
Osek, 70, 85, 100
Oserchiume, D'Jeghen Pasha Dondar, 62

Osman I, 127
Ottoman Army, 57–58, 62, 65–66, 68, 70, 73, 94, 96–97, 99–101, 140–42, 144, 148–49, 151
Ottoman cavalry, 30, 151
Ottoman Empire, 5, 7, 52, 71, 73–74, 127, 134–36, 139, 142, 147, 149

P
Pasha, Ibrahim, 97, 99
Pasha, Mehmet, 65, 94
Pasha, Osman, 94
Pashalals of Romelia and Bosnia, 147
Pashala of Bosnia, 143
Pashala of Bosnia and Romelia, 142
Pasha of Aleppo, 85
Pasha of Anatolia, 61–62, 66, 85, 94
Pasha of Bosnia, 142
Pasha of Buda, 96
Pasha of Damascus, 61–62, 66
Pasha of Romelia, 61–62, 66
Pasha's Chiaja, 89
Pasha's Guard, 88
Pasha's pages, 88
Patacin, 75, 93, 101, 103
Patakin, 24
Peace of Karlowitz, 42, 113, 125, 142–43, 148–49
Peterwaradein, 80, 82, 94, 104, 132
Philippopolis, 85
pioneers, 77, 108, 112
Poland, 106, 141–44, 149
Porte, 25, 28, 30, 52, 84, 86, 97, 115, 117, 127, 129–31, 139, 141–45, 147–48, 151–52
Procurator Morosini, 128–29
Prophet Mohammed, 74, 95, 112

R
Raab, 97, 99, 140
Republic of Venice, 127–28
risdales, 8, 11, 32, 50, 136, 148–49

S
sabers, 13, 17, 33, 105, 111
sabre, 18, 152
Salie-Pasha Cialcagy, 94
Sea of Marmara, 85, 127, 130
selictar, 88–89
Serakuli Infantry, 58, 62–63, 74, 89
Serasker, 52, 58, 61–63, 66, 75, 77–78, 80, 85, 91, 94–95, 100–101, 103–4, 141

Serasker Arat Pasha, 103
Serasker Cimengies Pasha, 78
Seratkuli, 11, 139
Seratkuli Cavalry, 15
Seratkuli Infantry, 11, 61
Seratkuli Militia, 137, 142–43, 148
shields, 13, 15, 152
siege of Belgrade, 26, 106, 117, 132
siege of Candia, 19, 22, 106, 108, 110–13, 115
siege of Naisel, 118
siege of Peterwaradein, 132
siege of Siclos, 73
siege of Strigonia, 100
Siege of Szigetvar, 154
siege of Vienna, 31, 36, 50, 53, 108, 111, 113, 134, 138, 141, 148
sieges of Buda, 93, 99, 117–18
siege to Belgrade, 123
siege to Kamieniec, 106
Sipahi, 108, 151–52, 154
Slankamen, 9, 36, 42, 78, 80, 94, 104, 131
Slankamen campaign, 9
Slavonia, 70, 85, 142
Sophia, 9, 85, 94, 103
Standard, Mohammed, 50
stirrups, 32–33, 88–89
Suleiman Pasha, 95
    great Vizier, 100
Suleyman, 57, 94, 108, 149
Suleyman Pasha, 59, 68, 70, 73, 75
Suleyman Pasha of Bosnia, 94
Sultan, 9–10, 36, 41, 57, 84–85, 101, 104–5, 128, 130, 136, 138, 140, 142, 148–49
Sultan Mahomet, 66, 73
Sultan Mahomet IV, 9, 127, 148
supplies, military, 68, 91

T
Tartar corps, 99
Tartar Guards, 62
tartars, 15, 30, 32–33, 35–36, 52, 65–66, 68, 73–74, 92–94, 96–97, 100, 139, 141, 143–44, 146–47
tefterdar-pasha, 62
three-tailed pashas, 39
Timar Cavalry, 36
timariots, 53, 61, 99, 108, 147
Toprakli, 12, 138–39, 148
Toprakli Cavalry, 38, 58, 61, 63, 65, 68, 73, 92
Toprakli Infantry, 68, 108, 117
Toprakli infantrymen, 117
Toprakli Militia, 136–40, 142, 147
Transylvania, 30, 57, 73, 84, 86, 97, 101, 104–5, 135, 142, 144
Transylvanian Cavalry Corps, 99
troops, tributary, 138–39
Turkey, 5, 30, 128, 134

Turkish and Tartar Harnesses, 33
Turkish army, 5, 30, 36, 41, 50, 57, 93, 100, 103, 141, 147
Turkish Azap Infantrymen, 153
Turkish camp, 50, 59, 62, 65, 70–71, 73, 77, 80, 82, 101, 140
Turkish cannons, 22, 70, 80
Turkish entrenchments, 70, 77, 80–82, 103, 120, 122
Turkish Fleet, 127, 130, 132, 145

V

Venetian fleet, 113, 131, 145
Venetians, 106, 108, 111–12, 127–31, 141–42, 144–47, 149
Venice, 25, 52, 127–29
Vienna, 5, 36, 41, 50, 52–53, 57, 73–74, 84, 91–92, 96–97, 99, 107–8, 111, 113, 140–41
  besiege, 52, 85, 92, 99, 106
  besieged, 58, 65, 100
Vienna Campaign, 96, 140
vivandiers, 53, 111, 148
Vizier, 9, 36, 38, 41, 57–58, 78, 80–82, 92–94, 96–97, 99–101, 104, 106, 108, 128–29, 131
Vizier Kiuperly, 59, 86, 91, 94, 131
Vizier Suleiman Pasha, 100
Vizier Suleyman Pasha, 71

W

Wallachia, 30, 50, 65, 86, 133, 142–44, 149
Wallachians, 62, 66, 74, 93–94
weapons, 13, 16–17, 19, 35, 92, 104, 111, 140

Z

Zegrin, 106, 113, 115
Zenta, 82, 84, 93–94, 104

Siphai in 1646 by Melchior Lorch